ON WRITING AND THE NOVEL

NOVELS BY PAUL SCOTT

ON WRITING
AND THE NOVEL

◆ ◆ ◆

ESSAYS BY PAUL SCOTT

◆

EDITED WITH AN INTRODUCTION
BY SHELLEY C. REECE

WILLIAM MORROW AND COMPANY, INC.

NEW YORK

Library of Congress Cataloging-in-Publication Data

Scott, Paul, 1920–
    On writing and the novel.

    Includes index.
    Contents: Imagination in the novel—Aspects of writing—Meet the author : Manchester—[etc.]
    1. Scott, Paul, 1920–   —Authorship.   2. Fiction—Authorship.   3. India in literature.   I. Title.
PR6069.C596Z466   1987   824'.914   86-19260
ISBN 0-688-06909-6

Printed in the United States of America

First Edition

1 2 3 4 5 6 7 8 9 10

BOOK DESIGN BY PATRICE FODERO

To Mary

CONTENTS

◆

On Writing and the Novel

ACKNOWLEDGMENTS

◆

My thanks to Mrs. Nancy Edith Avery-Scott, Paul Scott's widow, and Mr. Bruce Hunter, authors' agent and director of David Higham Associates, for permission to gather, edit, and print these essays. My further thanks to the staff, especially Caroline Swinson, in Special Collections at McFarlin Library, University of Tulsa; to the Oregon Committee for the Humanities, which awarded me a Summer Travel Grant in 1982; and to the Humanities Research Center, University of Texas, Austin. Thanks also to Liz McKinney, who helped me locate the Scott papers, and to Marlene Mahoney, who introduced me to Scott's fiction. My grateful appreciation to colleagues in the English Department at Portland State University, whether actively teaching or recently retired, for their generous, friendly encouragement. Thanks to friends in Sheridan, Wyoming, and Lincoln, Nebraska, for their moral support. Finally, thanks to all members of my family for their gentle urgings to complete this work.

INTRODUCTION

♦

When Paul Scott won the Booker Prize for fiction in November 1977, he was unable to travel from Tulsa, Oklahoma, to London in order to receive it because he was too ill with cancer to withstand the rigors of the trip. Instead, his daughter Carol accepted the five-thousand-pound award for him. Scott himself celebrated the occasion by drinking sparkling Catawba juice with Mildred Ladner, review editor of the *Tulsa World,* in his Tulsa apartment. Those attending the awards dinner at Claridge's were denied not just Scott's presence, but any opportunity to hear him make a gracious, articulate acceptance address. Since Scott ordinarily prepared a fully written text for such occasions, an even larger audience of future readers was to be denied an extended statement about his vocation as a fiction writer.

After he won that prize for his last novel, *Staying On,* Scott began to be recognized as a significant novelist of his time. The sale of his later novels increased literally tenfold; *Staying On* was made into a film with Trevor Howard and Celia Johnston in the lead roles; Granada Television adapted *The Raj Quartet* for a thirteen-week series, *The Jewel in the Crown,* which became a popular success both in England and in the United States. Though Scott would probably not altogether have approved, he

11

has become part of a cultural phenomenon now called the "raj revival."

But for seventeen years before he was awarded the Booker Prize, Scott was already keeping what he called "my daily appointment with the muse," a phrase he adapted from Henry James to embody his sense of obligation to his work. Scott lived by that obligation: According to his own account, he spent six-and-a-half hours a day on his writing. Besides composing thirteen novels, Scott also wrote plays, literary and popular reviews, and essays which he delivered as lectures. Still, except perhaps for his fiction, there remains today a dearth of information about Scott's work.

During these seventeen years, Scott accepted more than a score of speaking engagements, with his audiences ranging from children at the Stamford Grammar School, Lincolnshire, to undergraduates, graduates, and faculty at the University of Bombay in India. His usual habit for preparing such addresses, informal or formal, was to write a holograph manuscript; revise it at the typewriter, often more than once; and finally to make innumerable handwritten revisions on the final typescript, sometimes to the point of illegibility.

Fortunately, Scott had an archivist's instinct: After he had given one of these lectures, he would keep the full text of his remarks, perhaps his concession to a belief in the writer's vocation or even to his sense that the essays would be important in the future. As a result, most of the texts remained among his papers at the time of his death—unknown to scholars, untouched in the McFarlin Library at the University of Tulsa until 1982, when they were gathered to be collected and printed in this volume.

He did not, however, always compose a complete text for his audience. No text remains from his 1959 lecture at the Writers' Summer School, Swanwick; from his National Book League lectures of 1963 and 1965; or from his talk at the Yorkshire Literary Luncheon of 1967. When he gave a talk about writing at Stamford Grammar School in 1975, he produced only notes and no full text. Occasionally, even if he did produce a text, part of it became lost somehow. For that reason, "Imagination in the Novel," given at the national Book League in 1961, remains incomplete.

In this collection are nine complete essays, one partial essay, and one set of notes. All were delivered after Scott had resigned from the David Higham Agency in 1960 to become a free-lance writer. "Imagination in the Novel" was delivered before Scott began writing *The Raj Quartet*, and the Stamford Grammar School talk after he had finished the last volume. The decade of 1964–74, the time of his work on *The Raj Quartet*, also marks the time of these essays.

The essays themselves embody a considerable range in subject and reference. Two of them tell about Scott's life, from recollected moments of childhood film making to recounting his adult writing habits. Three other essays reveal his politics— and his frustrations with English attitudes toward India, his feelings about the need to give international aid, and his belief in writing as an act of dissatisfaction. Six essays give directly his views on art—his discussion of the "imprisoning form" of the novel, his definition of fiction as a series of images, his recounting of his method of discovering and following the originating image for *The Jewel in the Crown*, commentary about his use of a narrative device for and the structure of *The Raj Quartet*. Throughout the essays, he reveals his ideas about history and its relation to the arts in a time of political flux.

Scott believed that authors live uneventful lives, so their biographies are of little consequence to readers. On that subject, he quoted William Faulkner, who thought that the biography of a novelist ought to consist of one sentence: "He wrote the novels and he died." Yet Scott did show interest in letting the public know about his life as an author, especially as particular moments of his biography illuminated his own development as a novelist. In "Meet the Author: Manchester" (1967), he relates with wit some facts about his family and himself; he describes his daily writing habits; and he explains why he writes about India, a subject which a number of English citizens saw with considerable indifference. "A Writer Takes Stock" (1972) is a biographical gem in which Scott accounts for his early life, beginning with his passion for film making from age nine to thirteen: He wrote scripts for films that took six months for his brother Peter and him to produce and that lasted as long as an hour in performance. He also tells more about his family background: his father's career as a commercial artist, his aunt Florrie's as an artist's assistant, and his mother's as a part-time model. Further, he recounts some incidents during his schooling at Winchmore Hill Boys School, from which his father had to remove him when the Great Depression hit the Scott family in 1934. Although Scott became an accountant, he still thought of himself as an artist—first a poet, then a dramatist. He even had begun a novel by age eighteen. His novel, *Rachel*, was short-lived: His heroine never came on the scene. "A Writer Takes Stock" brings Scott through the war years to his job as an accountant from 1946–50, his employment by David Higham, and on to his career as a free-lance writer, beginning at age forty. This fascinating account may help readers to understand some origins of Scott's talent as a creator of character, scene, and narrative, as well as Scott's sense of his own vocation as novelist.

Scott openly reveals his political views in "Enoch Sahib: A Slight Case of Cultural Shock" (1969). Enoch Sahib, a caricature of Enoch Powell, serves as an emblem for those people with "a readiness to withdraw from the problems of the modern world," particularly international problems related to racial prejudice. Scott uses words like "torpor," "inattention," and "insularity" to dramatize the English lack of interest in things Indian. He writes of a few incidents from his 1964 journey to India in order to show how Indian warmth and hospitality towards him aroused the suspicions of the English sahibs and memsahibs at drinks and meals.

Finally, and most important for Scott's politics and his fiction, he tells of his visit to a remote Indian village, in order to show how the fear of strange and alien customs among people not one's own became a threat even to Scott's deepest liberal humane beliefs. He experienced cultural shock himself in that isolated village—the only Englishman there, forced into the role of a sahib by his host. When he returned to an urban hotel, he became ashamed of his ingratitude and shame, but didn't let himself stay in this insular comfort. That very comfort, Scott suggests, leads to the kind of moral decline which Enoch Sahib encourages.

In "Literature and the Social Conscience: The Novel" (1972), Scott explores the artist's relation to society. He disassociates politics from art, in the sense that he doesn't believe an artist should use a novel to make a political statement. After quoting Shelley on poets as the "unacknowledged legislators of the world," Scott says that he wishes Shelley had kept his mouth shut. Scott's own way of approaching the subject is to ask, "To what is the writer in *the last resort* committed?" For Scott, the answer, finally, involves the importance of "mystery" rather than "statement," of exploring through his art what he doesn't know rather than preaching in his art from dogmatic certainty.

And yet, for Scott, literature has always been a literature of dissent, art that begins with the artist being unsatisfied with life. Scott identified racial prejudice as the major political problem at the time he delivered this essay as a lecture in India; still, he was unwilling to say that writing about that subject would make one novelist better than another. He claimed that he was only trying to define his own way of looking at novels, and he made no claims for other novelists. For him, the importance of mystery remains.

In "After Marabar: Britain and India, A Post-Forsterian View" (1972), Scott suggests that E. M. Forster's *A Passage to India* was not the final word about British and Indian relationships. Then he elaborates his own reasons for writing about the end of the raj as a time of declining imperial certainty among the

English people. An anecdote from his 1969 visit to India becomes emblematic. When an Indian asked Scott, "What do you think you have to offer the world *today* that might be of value?" Scott was unable to provide an immediate answer, and before he saw this same Indian again, three days had passed. His answer at that time was that the uncertainty that he had anything of value to offer might itself be of value. Scott held to this idea of the importance and persistence of uncertainty, especially in the period after imperial England had imposed its national personality on others. Scott considered his novels a form of moral dialogue between writer and reader, one in which the writer says, "This is right, isn't it?" and the reader, in the manner of F. R. Leavis, says, "Yes, but. . . ." Scott believed that the English were largely ignorant about India—about the way it was acquired and administered, in addition to the way it contributed to the well-being of England. Further, he believed that the English were largely ignorant of policies in force in the ruling of India. He believed, finally, that his fiction would help to reduce the weight of that ignorance and consequently of prejudice. He wrote about that India of the past in light of the present, "leaning its weight on the vanished world I attempt to illustrate, as if it is looking for an extra source of inspiration."

These essays on politics do overlap with Scott's views on art, particularly those in which he considers writing more generally. In "Aspects of Writing" (1965), the occasion of lecturing to an audience of amateur and professional writers at the Writers' Summer School, Swanwick, determined the need for his remarks to be somewhat general. He solved this problem first by being entertaining and second by seriously examining a time of uncertainty in England, 1945–65, that influenced writers' works. Writers are confused by the social scene, and their works show this confusion, since writing is a social art. Scott looks at the presence of sex in fiction as a subject deriving from this uncertainty—sex as something we all know we have, regardless what little we may know about anything else. He also considers those twenty years as an age of disenchantment with established processes that had been perfected by 1945. He recognizes the presence of novels of transition like John Braine's *Room at the Top* and David Storey's *Flight into Camden*, which compares an older working-class generation with a younger educated class. But he finally encourages all the participants at Swanwick to engage with vitality in seeking new definitions for the time which they live and write.

"The Architecture of the Arts: The Novel" (1967) explores a series of critical concepts including "The Novel," "form," "function," and "reality." In this lecture, Scott calls into question some of the contemporary critical statements that have been written about these concepts. Further, he questions some of the innovative writing in fiction—particularly B. S. Johnson's loose-leaf novel and Julio Cortázar's *Hopscotch*. He moves then to Walter Allen's definition of the novel as "an extended metaphor of the artist's view of life," a definition used on other occasions in these essays. Considering form to be limited by the physical materials out of which novels are made, Scott also moves to discuss "the prison in which novels are confined"—that is, the book—as their form; here he adopts Bernard Bergonzi's definition of a novel as a "small, hard rectangular object whose pages are bound along one edge into fixed covers, and numbered consecutively." The function of novels, he concludes, is to convey a view of human reality. Scott believes that images, the primary material of novels, contain that view, and, once encoded into language and put into the form of a book, they become edifices for human use.

When Scott won an award for *The Towers of Silence*, his acceptance remarks, "The *Yorkshire Post* Fiction Award" (1971), extended several themes that he had articulated in other essays. One such theme is the way scholars persist in discovering the irrelevant or the already discovered. Here Scott cites the case of two scholars arguing over who found out that the original Lord Jim of Joseph Conrad's novel by that name was Augustus

Podmore Williams, something which had already been discovered and was possibly not worth knowing. Scott also ridicules the way that government scientists had been analyzing novels with computers, particularly when they discovered that the authorship of works by Ian Fleming and Graham Greene was questioned because there was too much variety for either of these writers to have written one of his own works. In this way, Scott reintroduced the need for an author to explore mystery in human experience and to make the novelist's work an attempt to create joy, both for the writer and the reader.

Other essays about art turn more directly to Scott's own creative process and to both *The Birds of Paradise* and *The Raj Quartet*. "The Architecture of the Arts: The Novel" has already shown how crucial a central image is to the writing of fiction. Both "Imagination in the Novel" (1961) and "Method: The Mystery and the Mechanics" (1967) discuss the way in which a central image affected Scott, and each elaborates his method of exploring it.

Scott begins "Imagination in the Novel" by presenting "an image, a dumb charade, for instance a woman appearing in a doorway." The essay immediately explores the details of the image—both the woman and the doorway in which she appears. The woman is beautiful, yet she holds herself as if exhausted, possibly unwell; the doorframe might be of bamboo.

Scott discovers in this "tentative doodling" that this image is abortive; still it leads to the idea of "fine feathers," and soon to the idea of "the birds of paradise" as "a thing that glitters." He researches the image, finding out what he can about those birds, and the knowledge heightens his imagination. He discovers a central image consisting of several elements—a man, a woman, an Indian prince, the birds of paradise, and the end of something. Much of the rest of this unfinished essay, including a quotation from the final section of *The Birds of Paradise*, embodies the way Scott went about exploring threads of possibility in a complex image.

INTRODUCTION

With "Method: The Mystery and the Mechanics," Scott defines a novel as "a sequence of images," then says, "In sequence these images tell a story." For him, the story and its order do not come first; "The images come first." He discusses the historical and political scene in India on which his narrative is built as factual, referring to specific events in Amritsar, 1919, and in the Quit India campaign, 1942. Then he tells of his return visit to India in 1964, a trying visit which included ten days in a remote village in Andhra Pradesh. Scott recalls that the specific image came floating into his mind "as images always do—apparently by chance, unexpectedly—in the dark of a restless, sleepless night." And this image, Scott's "prime mystery," was "a girl, in the dark, running, exhausted, hurt in some way, yet strangely of good heart—though, resilient. Her face and figure a sense rather than an observed condition. But she runs." Scott came to feel that she represented "something admirable in the human spirit." He also compares this image of a girl, by now given the name Daphne Manners, to a circumstance of 1919: A mission school superintendent, Miss Sherwood, had been dragged from her bicycle and beaten in Amritsar at that time. Then—approaching this central image from the back, using a "technique of reverse exploration," "of comparison"—Scott discovered his fictional mission school superintendent, Miss Edwina Crane, the main figure in the first section of *The Jewel in the Crown*. The technique Scott developed through the images of Miss Manners and Miss Crane—exploration through comparison—became a focal technique, not just for *The Jewel in the Crown*, but for the whole of *The Raj Quartet*. In composing all four novels, one character or version of an incident in the novel is compared with another to deepen the mystery of people and events in India, and to engage the reader in the moral dialogue to which Scott refers directly in "The Architecture of the Arts: The Novel." In this way, the reader is kept a little off balance, being constantly denied certainty, and the novels remain dynamic.

19

"After Marabar: Britain and India, A Post-Forsterian View" (1972) affirms this discussion of the central image through a brief statement about Miss Barbara Batchelor, the focal character of *The Towers of Silence*, and herself a retired missionary, one who taught at the mission school in Muzzafirabad just after Miss Crane had left that job. Clearly—from the similarity of their circumstances, their characters, and even their luggage— Miss Batchelor and Miss Crane are to be seen in relation to each other in just the same way Scott states that Miss Crane and Miss Manners should be compared.

While several essays refer to single novels from *The Raj Quartet*, Scott's talk at the Stamford Grammar School (1975) provides readers with nearly his only words about the entire tetralogy; his only other comments appear in a few of his letters to his editor at William Heinemann, to some admirers of his fiction, and to one graduate student writing a dissertation in the United States. Though Scott made only notes for this talk, they both illuminate his work and provoke the reader to wonder further. The notes identify May 1964 as that moment in which a remembered incident in his recent return to India was transformed into fiction for *The Jewel in the Crown*. At that time, an Australian woman and an Indian man about whose affair Scott had heard, became Daphne Manners and Hari Kumar in 1942. They were consciously compared with people in the Amritsar incident of 1919 and the visit to India in 1964. Further, Scott identifies the narrator as a "stranger or traveller," one who has gathered interviews, letters, extracts from works or accounts written or tape-recorded by the characters. The novel itself is the writer's own "reconstructions" from those documents. Scott identifies himself as "not quite" the writer—in that way, he can achieve both detachment and involvement for the purpose of narration.

Scott states in his notes that he had no idea that there would be four novels when he began *The Jewel in the Crown*. This view is affirmed by the first of his holograph notebooks for

The Raj Quartet: on the first page of the first notebook, Scott writes " 'Risk all': the Indian novel I ought by now to be able to write."

The majority of the remaining notes focus on the other three novels in *The Quartet*. *The Day of the Scorpion* is identified as, on the whole, a reconstruction of events by the man travelling around India and England and collecting information from people. This novel, then, is a piece of "ordinary narration." The notes indicate, too, that this novel opens out politically in three ways: with a Congress Muslim (Mohammed Ali Kasim); with a military family (the Laytons); and with princely India (the setting of Mirat and the character of the Nawab). Then *The Towers of Silence* narrows down to the central consciousness of a single person, Barbara Batchelor, a retired missionary similar to Miss Crane, Barbie's predecessor in the Muzzafirabad Missionary School. At last, Scott is left with the problems of *A Division of the Spoils*. He felt that he needed to let in some "fresh air" by introducing new characters, particularly Guy Perron and Lieutenant Purvis. he felt, too, that he needed a slightly cynical tone to dramatize the English ignorance of India, and that he needed to convey the political–historical movement of the final novel without appearing to write just history. And last, he needed to round off the imagery of the novel. He solved that last problem by creating the poet Gaffur and by embodying the novel's imagery in Gaffur's poem at the end of *A Division of the Spoils*.

After this first section of the lecture, the notes become too epigrammatic for readers to decipher what Scott might be doing. Yet the question with which he begins that second section helps one to see the direction in which Scott's talk was to turn: "Why do I write about India?"

This question recurs as a theme in Scott's other essays. It is one about which he has intimations of an answer and yet one which he wants constantly to explore. Scott's time in India, 1943–46, was a watershed in British–Indian history, one that made his arrival and departure both too late and too early—too late for the time of Amritsar (1919) or the beginning of the Quit India campaign (1942), and yet too early for independence and partition (1947).

Some of the prominence Scott gives to this idea of history in his work is embodied in repeated use of Ralph Waldo Emerson's essay "History"—in his letters, his essays, and his fiction. The central quotation is "Man is explicable by no less than all his history." Scott has Barbara Batchelor discover this sentence in a book of Emerson's essays; then he uses "her tin-trunk of missionary relics" as a compelling symbol for that history, both personal and universal—"luggage crammed with relics of achievement, of failure, of continuing aspirations and optimistic expectations." Scott sees that history as his own past, feels its weight, and senses its continuity.

In this way, each person is implicated in what Scott calls "the moral drift of history"; each person contributes to that history day by day in each action. The background of history and the foreground of fiction are intertwined in an inseparable way for Scott. As he writes in his holograph notebooks to *The Day of the Scorpion*, "Well, it is my obsession to tell stories. (Does it matter whether they are true? History is always being re-written. Once done with a fiction is inviolable. So.)" Each civilian and soldier, English or Indian, contributes to the history of the raj. The relationship between each person's work and life becomes paramount, for in that way, each human being in Scott's work contributes to that moral drift, and Scott's fiction becomes a part of the history it records. If fiction can become an agent of humanity's moral imagination in a period of political flux, then possibly Scott's fiction is the closest a reader might come to engaging in moral dialogue during a time of uncertainty, that time in which Scott believed the English people have lived since 1945, the year in which a member of Parliament is reported to have said, "We are the masters."

Scott may have had another, even more personal sense of history, the sense of a place in it for himself beyond his own time. The care he took to keep his papers in some order serves as evidence, however small, of this belief. With the man himself gone, scholars can only be grateful that his remaining work, published and unpublished, makes a tacit argument on its own that his talents as a writer were both broader and deeper than either the academic community or the general reading public has so far recognized.

Editor's Notes

Scott's essays have been edited in a manner that interferes with the text as little as possible. No unnecessary apparatus was added. Scott did not write obscurely; few footnotes were needed. Changes were made only when necessary to clarify the text. Typographical errors were corrected; punctuation was changed to help readers, since these essays were originally given as lectures and some of the punctuation was included for purposes of indicating pauses. Paragraphing was sometimes changed because of Scott's own extensive editing. These mechanical changes simply brought the essays more nearly in line with ordinary editorial conventions. Scott's typed and holographic interpolations were included in each essay. Brief introductory or concluding statements were omitted when they related only to the occasion on which an essay was presented as a lecture and not to the enduring reading of the work as an essay in its own right.

Finally, in two cases, more than one version of an essay was given as a lecture on different occasions. Those cases occurred with "After Marabar: Britain and India, A Post-Forsterian View" and "The Architecture of the Arts: The Novel." The first of these lectures was given on December 5, 1968, to the Fellows of the Royal Society of Literature; that version was subsequently published in *Essays by Divers Hands*, ed. Mary Stocks, new series, vol. xxxvi (London: Oxford University Press, 1970), pp. 113–132. It was then revised and considerably changed before being given on Scott's lecture tour of India in 1972. These major extensive changes made by Scott led me to choose the second version over the first.

In the case of "The Architecture of the Arts: The Novel," the essay was revised and shortened twice, to be given in India in 1972 and again at Swanwick at the Writers' Summer School, 1973, as "The Form and Function of the Novel." The second and third versions reaffirmed the statements of the first, and I considered that version the most fully made statement of the three and the most suitable for this collection.

IMAGINATION IN THE NOVEL

♦

["Imagination in the Novel" was presented as a luncheon talk at a meeting of the National Book League, November 22, 1961. Unfortunately, the final part of the text is missing. While both a holograph manuscript and Scott's typed notes are available to help construct a text, neither provides the missing conclusion. His notes do, however, make it clear that no more than a page of the typed text has been lost and that the unfinished quotation with which the present typescript ends is, quite possibly, the intended closing of the text.

Yet, even incomplete, this essay provides a sense of Scott's creative processes at the beginning of The Birds of Paradise in the same way that "Method—The Mystery and the Mechanics" does for The Jewel in the Crown. This essay helps clarify the way that a novel, for Scott, comes from a central image by means of fusing imagination and knowledge.]

You begin with an image, a dumb charade, for instance a woman appearing in a doorway. She seems to be acting out a phrase: The end of things, pictures seldom fail to be ideas. Perhaps it's the end of an affair, or even the end of her life, because she doesn't look very well once her face emerges and you can get something like a look at her.

On the other hand, she's quite pretty. It's the way she holds herself, as if exhausted, that makes her seem unwell; that, and the slight film of sweat on her forehead. But perhaps she per-spires because of the heat. The doorframe in which she stands might be of bamboo. This is a bit depressing, because if she represents a new novel it might mean setting it in the Far East again. You wanted to write a novel set in Spain. But in Spain she looks different. She acquires a new name, Dora, and the man who was probably in the room she was coming into through the doorway has acquired an identity. He's called Bill. I quote a section from an abortive beginning:

> Ice buckets of champagne at six shillings a bottle were being brought down to the beach when Bill and Dora first came to Palella. They arrived by boat, sailing into the horseshoe bay from the north, round a promontory of terracotta-coloured rock that was sucked and slapped by the blue waters of the Mediterranean. It was a clear hot day. Out to sea there was a breeze and a swell, but the surrounding hills kept the wind out and the heat in. The tourists were laid out on the sand, brown and limp like stripes of anchovy. The boat ground to a stop with its bows dug into the shingle, and Bill and Dora came ashore followed by fifteen pieces of luggage. Dora was dressed in white slacks and a white husky sweater. The men on the beach waited for her to turn sideways to them and were not disappointed either by her not doing so or by what they saw when she did.

Well, you've worked in the heat, and presently showed that underneath that attractive exterior all isn't well with Dora. Quote: "Words like date, time, soon, and later were not, to use their own language of the moment, okay words, but they would slip out and, having slipped out, had to be left to wriggle away like tiny worms making for cover."

And here's another quote: "Usually he did not care much what kind of clothes he wore. Just occasionally something would take his fancy and then he set about getting it with a singleness of purpose which now she found endearing. She had not always. 'It's me,' she sometimes cried in those days. 'Me. It's because you've only got me. It's not enough for a man.' "

And yet another quotation concerning the thoughts of Carmen, the woman who looks after Bill and Dora in the villa they have rented. Carmen has two fishermen nephews. "It was only in each other's company that they were gallant to Dora. Either of them, caught by her alone, would blush and stand awkwardly. This did not escape Carmen's notice. She knew there would be no trouble, but the boys were sixteen, and twins, and in male twins the passions of the sea could run strong. She prayed, just to be on the safe side, to the void which had replaced her girlhood image of the Holy Mother, and while she was at it she mentioned Bill and Dora but could not have said why."

In this tentative doodling, certain interpretations of the original dumb charade have been at work. Dora is ill, and Bill knows it. They don't use words like *time*. Carmen prays for them without knowing why. There is a feeling of their both being outcasts, because attractive as they are as a couple and— judging by all that luggage, well off as they seem to be—there is this business about Bill expending sudden energy on buying clothes and Dora's cry: "It's because you've only got me. It's not enough for a man." Bill is a man without an *occupation*.

Those quotations are, as I said, from an abortive beginning to a novel, and obviously you don't begin to write a novel until you think you know where you're going. The original dumb charade had been worked up in a certain way, and we won't bother with how, why, and what. It's enough to say that at the point where Carmen prayed to the Holy Mother the whole conception petered out. Somehow it wasn't viable. The only things that remained viable were these: Bill as a man with no occupation, Dora as a woman who had come to the end of something. And a new thing, a new idea, embodied for the moment in the conception of Bill and Dora as extraordinarily attractive specimens. Fifteen pieces of luggage in itself suggest a concern with the splendor of their personal appearance. They wear, it could be said, fine feathers. Fine feathers. This whole business of the imagination is like an adventure, a mysterious trip up a fictional Amazon to find its fictional source. Again I quote from another abortive beginning, but one that actually portrays how the next image arrived, fairly quickly in the wake of the idea of fine feathers. "A concern grew in me to see the birds of paradise. I can't remember just what began it. It was probably the name itself, swinging up in the dark of a sleepless night and hovering there like the bar of a trapeze, pausing fractionally for the grasp of my comprehension before sweeping down and away, taking me with it into the fabulous world where the birds called and mated."

A man may turn up, a woman appear in a doorway. Sometimes this thing that glitters appears, sometimes it doesn't. The thing that glitters is often a symbol. If the symbol can be justified, it is best to use it for all it is worth, to be honest about it, to say: "This is my symbol and this is what it means." I dislike symbols that remain obscure. I fancy my leg is being pulled or that the author isn't himself sure of his symbol. Either way his illusion suffers.

It was the idea of birds of paradise that glittered, and they became my symbol because, upon investigation, they not only stirred me with the idea of their beauty, but yielded information pertinent to the idea of the woman in the doorway and to the general climate of something having come to an end. Research brought knowledge. At this stage it isn't enough to float upon the surface of the Amazon. You have to get up above the roof of the surrounding forest and see where it is you are.

The birds of paradise are found mainly in islands off New Guinea. I haven't been to New Guinea. I haven't seen the birds of paradise. This, in a sense, is irrelevant. One is not a reporter. I go, ridiculously, this said, to the Natural History

Museum and find there a glass cage of stuffed birds of paradise. A kindly and efficient Mrs. Pope there gives me the lists of books and published articles. In Hatchard's I discover on the second-hand shelves a rare and rather expensive two-volume work of travel by Alfred Russel Wallace (1823–1913), who was an authority on the subject. In the tropical bird house of the Regents Park Zoo I find a living bird, a specimen of the type called Princess Stephanie: black, with a shining emerald throat and tail plumes over two feet long. After staring at it for half an hour, I go to the parrot house and am entranced by the singing of a parrot that comes from Paraguay, and whom I call Melba because her trill has a coloratura quality. On the way out I meet a white peacock that erects its fan and, when sitting on the grass, reminds me of a Viking ship at anchor. In the cat house I watch a tiger and go later to Whipsnade [Zoo] to watch a tiger in more natural surroundings. I have watched tigers many times, but this time I seem to be doing it with a purpose; but do not yet know why. It is enough to say that the animal kingdom has become relevant to the job on hand. I tell my friends I am interested in the birds of paradise. One rings me up and draws my attention to a passage in a book she knows I have a copy of because it is written by an old and mutual friend. This passage, long forgotten, perhaps twelve years forgotten—comes at me with an air of melancholy, but that may be because I am consciously looking for anything that will illustrate this idea of something having ended, having been written off, finished, thought of no account, misunderstood, yet held on to. Held on to by Dora or by Bill or both. Here is the passage: "They are styled birds of paradise because when first discovered various and most extravagant fables were reported concerning them; amongst which, it was long generally believed, that whence they came or whither they went was unknown; that they lived on celestial dew; they were perpetually on the wing, taking no rest but in the air, were never taken alive, and consequently could only be obtained when they fell dead upon the earth; so that the vulgar, imagining them to drop out of Heaven or Paradise, and, being struck with the beauty of their shape and plumage, bestowed on them the singular name by which they are still distinguished."

"Were never taken alive" and "could only be obtained when they fell dead upon the earth." Those were the words that interested me most. Those and the information got from other sources that the natives of the islands where they were found always cut their legs off before selling the skins to Malayan, Chinese, and European traders, in order to provide evidence of their celestial origin, because if a bird had no feet, where would it perch? If it did not perch it obviously spent its life-span in flight. It was supernatural but not immortal. A connecting link, it struck me, between heaven and earth. A symbol, perhaps, of what people wanted to believe—not religiously—but about possible splendors in the midst of ugliness, magnificence among the damned.

Quite clearly now, the doorway at which this woman appeared gave on to a tropical scene; and also suggested, because of the birds, an island. Bill and Dora were together on an island, outcasts still, but no longer with fifteen pieces of luggage. The birds wore feathers bright enough for them all. The perspiration on Dora's face brought it into greater relief. Lines appeared on it. Certainly she is middle aged.

But how romantic—this idea of a man and a woman on an island, surrounded by birds of paradise. How romantic, how unlikely, how false. Dora isn't there at all. Only Bill is there. Why? And where is Dora? What is the connection between them? Whatever it is that has come to an end, it is over. They were together once. When? In the war? Could they have lived together on a houseboat in Kashmir? I have always wanted to write a book in which a man and woman came together on a houseboat on the Bagin Bagh. But Kashmir won't do. My experience of it was too short. The feeling of the Kashmiri landscape is too shadowy.

India. But I remember the tiger, and the peacock; and the white peacock now emerges in a picture of the garden. It is instantly romantic this time. Disenchantment plays no part in this picture of the garden with a white peacock erecting its fan amidst emerald green grass and indigo blue shadows. Were birds of paradise native to India, there would be birds of paradise in the treetops. But the only birds of paradise there can be are dead birds, bits of the birds, plumes in the headdress of a prince. An Indian prince.

An Indian prince. They still call them princes, but they have all been divested of their power since the British went. Their feet, you could say, have been cut off. You know something about the princes. You used one as a minor character in an earlier novel. You have always been interested in their changed fortunes. While the British ruled, the princes were kept going in all their feudal magnificence. Their fine feathers were kept shiny. But when the British went and all their lands were merged with the lands of the new dominion, they appeared, you might say, in their true light—they had been dead all the time, stuffed like the birds in the glass cages in the central hall of the Natural History Museum.

This is an exaggeration. From a generalization you work back to a particular truth; and while you are doing that the procession of mental pictures goes on. The garden in which the white peacocks strut is the garden of a palace. You can see it through the spaces between the thick boles of big trees. By moonlight it is of icing sugar beauty. In the daytime, flaking stucco and crumbling stone give it a look of decay. It could be a world of extremes; of splendors and magnificence, ugliness and damnation.

And here the imagination, spurred on by the excitement of finding how relevant the symbol is proving to be in relation to the original picture and its apparent meaning, here the imagination takes leaps and jumps which are impossible to recall. Was it on top of a bus, going once more to the Natural History

31

Museum, and thinking of the tiger, that the picture of Dora and Bill, *as children,* first appeared? Dora and Bill in white shirts, jodhpurs, and topees, watching a tiger, as I had done, but not from the safety of the other side of a set of iron bars: from a precarious position in a *machan,* built into the forked branches of a tree. I remember, though, when the idea of the cage first came. A wet June Saturday afternoon, at about four o'clock, staring at a white wall. It had an onion-shaped dome and bars wrought like latticework; once painted gold, but flaked and faded now. It was a big cage, big enough to have housed several fully grown giraffes. And hanging from its tin roof in simulated flight were stuffed specimens of the birds of paradise; below them, as a setting, the trees and shrubs of their natural forest. It was a fine cage; but also curious. The beautiful, ridiculous folly of a man rich enough to indulge an expensive fancy. An Indian prince. But of the old school. The grandfather, say, of the kind of modern prince who went to Harrow and played cricket for Bombay Province. And however symbolic the cage is to me, it is equally symbolic to the old Indian prince, because he had to joke about it. The birds were like the British: proud, convinced that they excited the admiration and wonder of all who saw them, but, in truth, stuffed, dead from the neck up and the neck down.

The princes were advised by Englishmen. The big states had what were called residents. The smaller states, sometimes grouped together for these purposes, were advised by what were called political agents. These men, agents and residents, represented the British Crown, which had certain powers over the states but would not otherwise much meddle in a state's internal affairs. The states were separated politically from what was called British India. They were self-governing. The Indian politicians of British India had no particular love for them. Few states were run on anything like democratic lines. The lasting monument to the perfidy of Albion is, to me, the way we pointed British India towards democracy but preserved through thick and thin the autocracy of the princes as if for all the world oceans separated them. But they were feudal islands in a democratic, socialist sea. And when we gave the Indians back their sea we left the feudal islands to their fate and, right up to the last few weeks, assured the rulers of those islands that no arrangement would be reached with British India for independence without there being princely consultation. This is something history will forget, if only because betrayal of undemocratic institutions like feudal kingdoms is never called betrayal. India has made progress. It is all free and democratic now. It is right that the feudal kingdoms should no longer exist. But to the novelist the smell of betrayal can never smell like roses. He is interested in people, and uncommitted to policies. How did it seem to the people concerned, those men of the political department, whose careers had been spent advising native rulers, encouraging them to rule their kingdoms well and be a credit to the British Crown which protected them. Might it not have seemed to some of them that their careers had been ill-spent that ended in betrayal from above? And read between the lines of recorded history and you find that the political department did not have much love for Lord Mountbatten's political bulldozer. Why? Because at least some of them knew that a way of life they had dedicated themselves to had come to an end. They, too, perhaps, appeared at doorways to survey the ruins of their public lives, unable to meet the eyes of the maharajah they had encouraged, frustrated, loved perhaps, stood by, stood out against. Was there amongst them no man who felt dishonored? For a dozen who said, "Well, old boy, times change, you've got to be realistic," wasn't there one who was silent, packed his bags, folded his tent, and barely had the nerve to say goodbye?

Imagination is not enough. Knowledge is necessary. And an experience of the oddity of life. The imagination, the knowing, and the experience finally cohere into a pattern. Bill is too young, one feels, to have been a political agent himself. The political agent is his father. Bill grew up in India, close to the palace of the ruler his father advised. And as a child he knew this garden and the white peacock, and a girl called Dora with whom he went to hunt a tiger. And the idea of princes suggests a particular one, a boy who will be a prince, who inherits the title just in time to surrender all its powers. And there they are, the three of them, the Indian princeling, the boy Bill, the girl Dora, rowing across a lake to an island on which is set up this curious cage filled with stuffed birds of paradise. The Indian princeling knows about his grandfather's joke that the birds are like the British, but says nothing. Bill, who is an ordinary boy, and yet an extraordinary one because everything about his childhood conspires to make him believe that one day he will have to take up his father's task of helping these people live better lives, simply responds to the physical fascination of the birds. It is Dora, poor Dora, who sees the birds as tokens of all the wonderful things that will happen to her when she is a grown-up woman.

Obviously it is no part of my intention to tell you so much about a book that's not published yet that you'll either decide it's not worth reading or that you know it all anyway so needn't bother. And in one sense the work of the larger imagination is finished. The imagination from this point on is directed at filling in the past, the bit that happened before the book began, filling in the details, tracing histories, producing characters who are needed but who tend, through the imagination, to change the totality of the book by their own strong demands. And there is the sheer hard grind of finding the right words so that you can put one after the other, significantly, constructing a shape that will lead you from the beginning you've worked up to to the end that you originally imagined.

And here, in two passages at the end of the book, is the image as it has developed—the woman at the door—and the idea as it has concluded, of something having come to an end:

First, the picture of Dora—a woman of middle age now, in India. The narrator is Bill. He has not seen her for many years.

They are standing in the cage, looking at the birds of paradise, now falling into decay.

> The tangential lines at the corners of her eyes, with the yellowing patches on her neck, the husky, ragged, mem-sahib voice, became, briefly, focuses for my tenderness and acquired beauty, as did all the traces left upon her by her years, for her years were her life and I had loved her as a child. She laughed, pointed out the three perched female birds. "Poor things," she said, "The finer-feath-ered their cockbirds were the prouder they were and the higher they tried to fly but also their skins were more valuable, weren't they? They'd get their legs cut off quickest of all." She put two fingers of her left hand on-to her temple and rubbed, as if she needed cologne there to soothe a sudden ache. Her eyes had brightened, li-quified just perceptibly along the lower rims. Leaving the cage, our bodies brushed lightly together. Hers felt as hard as flint."

This, then, is the door that the woman appeared at—the door of the cage; coming out of it with Bill. She is married to a man whose family had served for generations in the Indian Army. All that ended at independence. Her body is as hard as flint because she is immensely saddened by the sight of the birds and all that they used to represent to her, but she has a long experience now of living with reality.

The last words are Bill's. He is thinking of his father, the ex-political agent, from whom he became estranged for reasons pertinent enough to the theme of the novel but not to this talk. He has learnt recently that his father—a cold, silent man—had stormed into a room where the maharajah he advised was being persuaded to sign a preliminary agreement of accession to the new Indian Dominion and denounced the agreement as "an instrument of a blackguardly policy of intending seizure and forfeiture masquerading as an . . ." [The remainder of this man-uscript is missing. Full typed notes of this essay, found with Scott's papers, suggest that the essay will come to closure within a typed page.]

ASPECTS OF WRITING

◆

["Aspects of Writing" is the text of Scott's opening address to those who attended the Writers' Summer School, Swanwick, in August 1965. His active association with this school lasted some fifteen years, during which time he was host to guest lecturers on two occasions and a lecturer himself four times. Although the text for the first lecture Scott gave there (1959) is missing, those for his second (1965), third (1967), and fourth (1973) addresses to participants remain. "Aspects of Writing" is the second of the four. Besides encouraging the participants at Swanwick as writers, Scott also addresses with considerable wit the "confusion of the last two decades [1945–65] in English letters," describes the uncertainty which that confusion has produced, and urges these writers to be vital in the larger context of their work. He invites them to be part of the redefinition of their world, a world in which he concludes that perhaps "nothing is sure, nothing is planned, nothing has yet been achieved of any lasting value."]

On your program you'll see I'm down to speak on aspects of writing. Aspects are a bleak substitution for prospects, but don't be too alarmed. The title was made deliberately vague so that I could think carefully about what I might most usefully say.

I suppose I have two main tasks. First, to welcome you and wish you luck, which is a pleasure. Secondly, to send you away

37

from this auditorium not only awake, but alive: the most desirable state for any writer to be in. By alive I do not mean capable of plunging into the swimming bath at five A.M., or playing a vigorous game of clock golf before seven, doing sitting-up exercises in the corridors of the garden house while waiting your turn in the bathroom, or eating a hearty breakfast and then arriving in this hall with a sharp pencil, a virgin pad, and a strained expression of expectancy. I mean alive to the world, to the times we're living in.

Once, after finishing a novel, I went out for a walk. It came on to rain. I cursed myself for having taken a walking stick instead of an umbrella. I reached home eventually, soaked and cross, and complained to my wife of my lack of foresight. She looked at me with that bemused expression of tender consideration authors become used to, and pointed out that what I held in my hand looked like an umbrella to her. It was.

Well, we are all absent-minded at times. But even so, we can be alive in the sense I mean. We can also be greedy, uncharitable, envious, and smug—all the things that human beings are. We can arrogate to ourselves a sense of superiority, because we are writers or even certain *kinds* of writers. But we mustn't imagine that we live in a world of our own—although part of our job might be to create other worlds for other people to inhabit for an hour or two. Note, I did not say for other people to lose themselves in. Writing is a discovery. It is a vitamin, not a drug.

This is my fourth visit to Swanwick. If I've learned anything from the first three, it is that one comes here, above all, to be encouraged. On the platform or in the hall; in luck or out of it; talented, promising, or just resolutely plodding, in the hope that someone will buy a poem or a story, or even an anecdote, a few lines about a childhood memory (or rather more lines about a middle-aged experience)—we all need to be encouraged.

For most, part of every year that encouragement has to be

dragged up by its bootstraps, by ourselves, from whatever private fund of determination and self-confidence we have. Here, at Swanwick, I like to think that it is, if not in the air exactly, then anyway external to us, capable of being tapped, like a sort of invisible petrol pump that puts a tiger in our tanks.

Always look words up in a good dictionary, even when you know what they mean. *Encourage*: OED—"embolden, incite, advise, promote, assist (commerce and opinion, etc.)." To judge by the program head we shall be well advised and ably assisted. With luck, some of us might even be promoted. May I therefore attempt, in this opening talk, to embolden and incite? According to the OED, *incite* means "to urge, stir up, a person, etc." Just as I've never met a lady or gentleman in general, neither have I ever met a person etc., but the image is clear enough. Here we all rank as such, because surely we are all open to incitement, urging, and stirring? Swanwick is an airy pasture. The food is good and wholesome. The grapes are on the vines, and the sap is rising in the sukebind. Heaven knows what will happen.

Swanwick is a retreat from immediate pressures of private work, from the hysteria of inflated expectations, from the depression of disappointment. But it must never be a retreat from reality. Rather, for a week, here we have the chance to regain a proper sense of it. To come out of ourselves and look at others, not just as writers but as people. It is a pity to waste the opportunity, a pity to gather exclusively in cliques and factions and categories—and age groups. The chance to mix with people who share our specialized interests is nice to have, but what about those whose interest, whose experience, whose attitudes do not seem immediately to correspond with ours? Plenty of opportunity is given for like to mix with like in the workshops and courses and study groups. There business can be got down to, not so much to find out how it is done, but to glimpse other ways than your own of doing it, and, if necessary, adjusting your technique to the point where it combines with your talent in a natural harmony and so produces something worthy of you, and therefore of other people's attention, which means, as a rule, something salable. One word of warning about the workshops and courses. We all know the famous definition of a camel? That it is a horse designed by a committee? Workshops exist to *help* you discover how to design your own horse. No one can *teach* you to do so. And it must always be your own horse. Better three hundred three-legged ponies than one giant four-legged, glassy-eyed, constipated dromedary.

But outside the workshops, I do suggest that you resist the temptation to seek out *only* those people who wear the same label and therefore look *safe*. Accept the element of danger. I don't mean that an elderly gentleman with a green label marked CRIME must—in order to secure my approbation—chase through the vegetable garden a nubile young lady wearing a white label marked POETRY. In this civilized world we live in there are many ways of making contact with other human beings that won't end up in a painful scene or in reproach and recrimination in the office of our infinitely understanding but much overworked secretary.

Sometimes, if you can, forget too that The Hayes is crammed to the roofbeams with people who write. It shouldn't be very difficult. Sometimes, looking at each other, we wonder if any of us actually *does*. Imagine instead, then, that it is alive with female and male specimens of the species *Homo sapiens*—people, if you like—from one of those nice plays about characters who are held up at a railway station or an airport waiting for a conveyance forward.

And this morning, just for a while, imagine if you can that none of you is English—because it is of writing in England, or Britain, in the last twenty years, roughly, that I really want to talk. Not just of writing in England, but of the English themselves. If I seem to use the novel as a sort of norm of reference, please forgive me. It is the only branch of writing I presume to know anything about.

Why *do* I want to talk about writing in England, and want

you to imagine, initially, that in this hall I alone am of that nationality? So that you can get the feeling of losing your English inhibitions? Yes—but the real answer is because I should like us all to leave this auditorium looking at each other as if we were friendly strangers met on some hospitable foreign shore, who have found, to our amazement, that we all come from the same place. So that when the time comes for us to go back to it, to get on with our same but different jobs, we shall have a clearer idea of the place we live in, having seen it briefly through eyes other than our own—an idea of other people's notions of what we might be up against, of what we can be led astray by, even of what we might be working towards.

This is the only way I know of speaking to you all, and the opening speaker has this basic obligation—to speak to you in the round: criminal people, romantic people, straight and narrow people, space people, play people, people who speak in rhyming verse and those who speak in blank; those for whom a couple thousand words are enough to make a point, those who somehow fail to make one in a couple hundred thousand. Quick writers, slow writers, halt and lame writers, those who write in the bath and those who are reluctant to take a bath at all; writers who write with pencils or pens, and those to whom the muse comes so fleetingly but with such urgency that an electric typewriter is scarcely a sufficient means of keeping up with her tyrannical dictation and getting it all down before she goes off for a quick one to revive her own flagging spirits.

To speak to you, initially, as a foreigner who tries to explain his society, to speak to you in the hope that by the time I've finished speaking you'll have recognized that this society is also yours.

Talents vary, interests diverge. Words are forever changing in weight and measure, which is why we should look them up to see how far we have deviated from the last recorded definition. What I can never ignore, when I sit down to write, is that I am someone born in my age, subject to its pressures, prejudices, and expectations, scorched by its past, living in its present, fascinated by its future. Literature has always had its roots in society. Examine a nation's literature and you come to a conclusion about the nation. I want to do this the other way round. Which is why I start with Britain, and the British.

Up until twenty years ago, most Britons had a good idea of what they were. Since then they haven't been so sure. Today, although a man might wake up feeling pretty British—thick-headed and stubborn and disinclined to speak to anyone to whom he hasn't been improperly introduced—by the time he has eaten his Danish Bacon and his Polish egg, drunk his Brazilian coffee or Indian tea, spread some Dutch butter and Spanish orange marmalade onto bread made from the flour of Canadian wheat and toasted under the grill of an oven manufactured by a Hungarian refugee who has off-loaded his unsalable stock onto the North Thames Gas Board, our Briton might be forgiven for feeling somewhat ambivalent.

By the time he has read the Dead Sea scrolls of his morning newspaper, and warmed to a photograph of the American president looking gravid with inherited liberal ideas, to one of Mr. Wilson looking like a small-property owner, to one of Mr. Heath looking hysterically distrait at the prospect of leading his party back to power, like a cheerful puppy to its own sad vomit—by the time he has had a good laugh at a picture of General de Gaulle, wearing his sleeve on his heart in order to kiss without contagion both Oriental cheeks of whatever anti-American general has emerged in the past three weeks as the one most unlikely to succeed—by the time he has regretted the empire, banned the bomb, shaken his head at some new proof of Tory financial manipulation and his fist at our present-day labor force for being a lot of ungrateful layabouts—by the time he has grunted approval of Parliament's intention to abolish hanging but to retain homosexuality—usually in that order—tottered to the station recalling the illusory days of his youthful athleticism, and caught the eight-fifteen to the city, where the pound is expected to survive for yet another day of fluttering uncertainty—he will have become fixed, like an exhausted chameleon, in the true colors of his workday persona—that of a man of slender means and some pretentions whose neighbors the Joneses no longer live just opposite but who crop up in all kinds of unexpected places like Washington, Zanzibar, Indonesia, and Smithwick.

Less efficient than the Germans, less rational than the French, less sophisticated than the Swedes, poorer than the Americans, paler-skinned than so many of his fellow members of the non-republican commonwealth who, as equally loyal subjects of his own sovereign lady, punch his ticket on the bus from Waterloo to Crutched Friars—he is hard put to it to know just where the corridors of his own power have led him.

Since man and society are emotionally inseparable, since power is what society is constantly in pursuit of as a means to happiness, and since literature is a celebration of man as a social animal, this perplexity of the modern Briton has to be recognized, even it if isn't fully understood, if we are to understand the currents that have led English writing in the last twenty years into—not a backwater, but certainly a complex of streams that look muddy and diverse, but which might add up to a delta of sorts.

The landscape—slightly to change the metaphor—the landscape of the written word, when at its best, is both diversified and rich. In times of social uncertainty the diversification increases, the richness thins out. When a generality of people know what they are, and what they have, and what they want, they are like an army concentrated in depth on a relatively narrow front. The writer has always been a man with his mind and heart set on penetration of such defenses—in the first instance of the series of outer perimeters: manners, customs, usage. Dealing with those appeals to his sense of fun. The inner, more serious objective challenges the seriously committed parts of his nature. But what he opposes must be clear to him. If it is clear to him it will also be clear to the defenders.

Movements in political and social history are, at an early stage, the dreams of writers. I do not mean that writers are lordly, powerful creatures who change our shapes for us at will. But, by and large, they are invariably representative of the collective discontent with established processes that leads to change and social development. And by the nature of their skills, they enjoy both the pleasure and the responsibility of making that discontent articulate and infectious.

So much of contemporary life seems at first to be merely amusing. One smiles and shrugs, having scarcely the heart even for what Mr. Angus Wilson calls gentle irony—which is how he summed up the attitude a modern English writer needs to adopt towards his available material.

The case of Angus Wilson is possibly symptomatic. He strikes me increasingly as a man with all the great traditional equipment of the novelist, but also as one who has found as yet no novel to write that is worthy of his talents. The same might be said of others, and perhaps they perfectly represent the age, an age of comment by imitation, rather than of creation by attack, of the short trot or cheap day excursion into the marginal country of local and broadly uninteresting custom. Walking the tightropes between our compulsion to speak and our search for something to say, perhaps we mostly seem to be playing. But then, to write in a major way about Britain today is not so easily done. It is as though one were expected to make a monument out of a Maypole.

Which image brings me back to other celebrations—those of 1945, the twenty-year-old date I had in mind when I said that up until then most Britons had a good idea of what they were. They had made some small but telling contribution to the subjugation of European Fascism, having given it some equally small but telling assistance from 1929 onwards. They also achieved in 1945, by a remarkable coincidence that left them breathless, a victory at home. In a khaki election the old anti-progressive guard was swept out of power and the new one swept in. Here was the milestone beyond which the road would lead to the elimination of social injustice, poverty, class consciousness, and imperial domination abroad.

Women were already emancipated. Achievement of this emancipation had been a long, hard haul—extending as far back, wouldn't you say, at least as Chaucer's portrait of the Wife of Bath? Which poem might have suggested to us that we can always leave the ladies to enjoy emancipation in private, even when it is denied to them in public. Which may be why Shaw's reputation—"Why can't a woman, Be more like a man?"—has diminished to that of someone who devised the book for a successful musical comedy.

And yet, what the ladies have done with their emancipation is a guide to what the British generally have done with their other reforms. Or rather, to what those reforms have done to them—led them, by and large, into a position of hard-fought-for-status they can't be sure is quite the one they had in mind.

But in 1945, everything seemed, if not won, at least established as the new norm. The welfare state began, and one felt that Dickens would have smiled approvingly. Europe, it is true, was in ruins, but at least totalitarianism lay apparently dead in the rubble—and Spender, Auden, and Isherwood were somehow vindicated. And with a Labour administration in power, the empire, that symbol of middle-class pretension and upper-class mercantile greed, was clearly destined to go for the Burton we all felt that Mr. Forster had always hoped it would.

But of course, although it would take a few years yet for us, as a nation, to become disenchanted with the consequence of our reforms, writers, even at this early date, were all of a sudden deprived of their traditional sources of reforming zeal and inspiration.

> When Adam delved and Eve span,
> Who was then the gentleman?

John Ball asked in the fourteenth century, and this is a question we can hardly fail to hear continually vibrating in most of the great works of creative writing from Chaucer through Shakespeare to Bunyan and on even unto Mr. Galsworthy—a question posed not in the narrow sense of *Who is Lord and Who is Master?* but in the broader sense of our general human sensibility. In any body politic there has always seemed to be both a head and a heart, the heart that now seems to be lacking, to be gone away, reduced by the unexpected pressures of the alarmed intellect reacting like one of Pavlov's dogs to a bell that has announced the end of the party and the beginning of the washing up.

> When Adam delved and Eve span
> Who was then the gentleman?

In his four-volume work, *English Social History*, G. M. Trevelyan described this ancient couplet as the most modern question of all. But he was writing in 1940 or 1941. He had not heard—because it was not made until 1945—the statement which somehow ended the hilarious party of traditional English radicalism. In that year, flushed as a laborer might be, not with toil but with the beer earned by the sweat of it, a certain Adam whose name I do not even remember, got up on his feet, in, I think, the House of Commons, and attempted to quell the Tory opposition with the memorable line, "We are the masters now." And from that moment, I think, the English stopped knowing what they were and writers stopped knowing what they were in honor bound to say.

I wonder whether the man who said, "We are the masters now" ever knew the extent of the damage he did, not so much to his party's image, but to the people's image of their own good nature and good intentions? But certainly he prepared for those further disappointments which, one by one, stripped us of the old skins of what we had hoped was our common humanity, and covered us, layer by layer, with skins of a different kind—those in which you usually see us dressed today: the skins of irony, satire, and triviality, of obsessive concern with the artifacts of so-called affluence. The skins of an equally obsessive concern with the marginal differences between new manners, customs, and scales of income; a kind of smug, wholly unserious, apparently supercilious attitude to the real business of making a go of life in this dangerous powder barrel we call the world.

But if these skins are so thin that we appear to outsiders as so many reflections of a time-expired emperor wearing no clothes, to us there is more the feeling of being naked because we had divided our cloak and given half of it to a starving beggar.

We have seen a lot in the last twenty years. We have seen the distinctions of class go into a kind of reverse, rather than into a decline. We have seen our voluntarily relinquished empire disappearing into the mists of territorial fragmentation and dangerous racial memory instead of arising into the reassuring morning of a commonwealth. We have seen the problem of color removed from countries that we used to classify as ones in which the natives were (a) friendly, or (b) not to be trusted, and translated into a problem that might win or lose an election here at home. We have seen the emergence of radical Tories in whom it is difficult to believe, and of reactionary socialists in whom it is all too easy to. We have seen grow up in our midst girls who—to the charitable motorist with a seat to spare and an eye for a lonely thumb—turn out to be boys, and boys who turn out to be girls, and those of them in whom the distinction never becomes clear, perhaps because, for these boys and girls of ours, there have been enough distinctions, and it is time to recognize that there are only, in the same powder barrel, human beings: human beings in need perhaps of redefinition.

And this, perhaps, is the point, which our children react to with a kind of flamboyant but witty native capacity for raw irony which the old and middle aged still seek sophisticated symbols of and clever explanations for.

So far, I have avoided using certain words and phrases: Alienation, The Existential Dilemma, Rebellion, Angst. The trouble with critics' words and phrases like these is that they become, as jargon so often does, more significant and meaningful than the state of affairs they are supposed to define. If we think of Alienation, or the Search for Identity—that old thing, which I'm alarmed to see coming back into the language of our Sunday culture—then we automatically think of it, because it sounds like a diagnosis, as a clue to a disease some clever person will presently find a cure for, leaving us meanwhile to enjoy suffering it. I far prefer to think of alienation merely as a question of knowing we no longer believe we know what is good for us. As human beings, we have never welcomed being told what is but have always preferred to work it out for ourselves, which is what we shall have to continue doing.

Meanwhile, English literature, reflecting the attitudes of a people who know what they know but also what they don't, can no longer be said to add up to anything like an attack in depth on the world as it is, because that world is no longer defended with anything like passion. Today, the battleground has a curious aspect. It is a sort of elongated front dividing from each other, those strange Gallup Poll creatures, the Nos and the Yeses who, to add to the confusion, frequently change sides. Behind, upon a comfortable patch of dry high ground, stand and sit the Don't Knows and Couldn't Care Lesses, like those polite, well-breeched Russians who during the Crimean War found some alleviation of their ennui in driving to the battlefield at weekends in open carriages, armed with parasols, binoculars, hampers of vintage Champagne and black caviar, to enjoy the fun of watching people making gallant fools of themselves.

From such a point of vantage they would see today little to excite them for long. An occasional, angry explosion, which, when the smoke has cleared, seems to have left whatever target it was aimed at quite intact; a skirmish or two between an attacking section of progressive light infantry and a well-entrenched company of old-fashioned dragoons, who have lost their weapons but retained their ideas of what is decent, whose anger is aroused in the main only at being interrupted in the serious business of preserving the status quo which really gave them a wretched time in childhood and early youth—so much so that they can't be blamed for claiming the benefits of it in their maturity.

Sex, for instance, is always good for a flurried exchange of ball and shot. One can appreciate why the subject of sex in this post-Freudian but pre-neo-Greek age should represent so great a proportional weight of the writers' armory. Clearly one cannot leave it at that noble, traditional English definition: "Ladies don't move," or at Mr. Beverley Nichols's youthful description of sex as "either a joke or a physical exercise." Nor can one rest content to leave the main subject of it crowned, as it were, with the flowers of Mr. D. H. Lawrence's romantic sensibility. On the other hand, one feels that the old dragoons may have a point or two in resisting its current literary ubiquity—and its tangential aspect—the use of certain words whose meaning we know, whose conveyed image might even be said to be familiar to us, to the point where we can only leave them to quit our daily language in order to inhabit exclusively our literature, but to burden it to the point where they must rank really as clichés, at all costs to be avoided. Asked, by one of our more distinguished publishers, who had made free with a blue pencil, to remove the last word of this kind from his otherwise promising first novel, a young writer, his eyes filling with unmanly tears, begged to be allowed to rescue this one last poor wretched refugee, saying, "If my book comes out without even one of them, how can I face my friends?"

To remain, for just a moment longer, on this no doubt boring subject (judging by your expressions), one might sum it up from the point of view of the parasoled, binoculared, don't-know-but-shocked spectators by describing a great deal of sex in modern literature as a smoke screen, from behind which the attacking writers hope to gain an advantage over the old guard, and the old guard, who feel quite capable of leading well-adjusted sex lives without assistance, retreat into prepared positions and wait for what they call the long-haired invader to fall, blinded by their own smoke, into the cesspool that lies behind the forward positions of any guard, old or new. In this world latrine duty is always laxly carried out, and even new brooms leave dust and dirt which eventually have to be swept under the carpet.

I think the reason why sex plays such a prominent part in modern literature is not so much that it is, as it were, being used as the tool that cuts out our old *romantic* notions of what men and women are—although this is one of its aims—but that sex is the one thing we all know that we have, at least in private. And the British not long ago proved that they even have it in *public*. And the case we are probably all thinking of reminds us of the fact that, to paraphrase Mr. Macmillan, some people obviously have it better than others, and turns our attention to a much more important subject—the all-important topic of Social Envy.

Mr. John Braine, the author of *Room at the Top*, was once criticized for loving what he pretended to hate. "The other evening," his hero, Joe Lampton, relates, "I found a photo of myself taken shortly after I came to Warley. My hair is plastered into a skullcap, my collar doesn't fit, and the knot of my tie, held in place by a hideous pin shaped like a dagger, is far too small. That doesn't' matter. For my face is, not innocent exactly, but *unused*. I mean unused by sex, money, by making friends and influencing people, hardly touched by any of the muck one's forced to wade through to get what one wants."

What Joe Lampton wanted was power.

Room at the Top was one of the first popular significant postwar novels—popular in the sense you know and significant in the sense I am talking about—because by forcing us to acknowledge what one critic called "the hungry snarl of youth," it also forced us to recognize that *power* was what we had lost, and what we felt we couldn't live without, although for the life of us we couldn't see what kind of power it would be both pleasant to wield and humanly reasonable to exercise.

But we wanted *in* again, wanted in on the extraordinary new world of purchasable artifacts—the first fruits of Tory-manipulated postwar, post-Socialist plenty—and this world of artifacts was one that Braine reminded us was there again for the taking, for the paying, and for the earning, if you could put out of joint the nose of the other man who wanted it. The ration book could be exchanged for the credit card, one with which you could buy what you felt you had earned as a member of an old civilization—a meal as nice as the defeated, liberated French were enjoying, although accompanied by a wine they would describe as vinegar in spite of its label saying Chablis, 1949. And you could buy and smoke a cigarette that distinguished you from the crowd, say State Express 555. And buy these things at a pleasant roadhouse, thirty miles out of the smoke, because really there was plenty of Saudi Arabian petrol somewhere to be had, and a car to put it in, if you slipped one sharply away from the export market—preferably a red convertible sports model—with its hood down in the rear and a pretty girl up in the front. And if she were the boss's daughter, and smelled of Chanel No. 5 (available then to those who had found a way of beating the personal travel allowance), so much the better. One was back in the illiberal world of dog eat dog.

Room at the Top was not published until 1957, but it relates to this earlier period; it is, in fact, *the* novel of the dawning age of affluence, because it maps the passions that led us into it. And of the *popular* novels of the twenty years we're considering, it probably ranks as one of the last consciously to attempt a connection with what Dr. Leavis calls "The Great Tradition." Many less-popular novels have continued to uphold it. I am thinking in particular of Mr. David Storey's novel *Flight into Camden,* which deals with another aspect of the end-result of our radical intentions—the gulf that appears between humble parents and their clever, state-educated children, although I also remember Mr. Storey proving something else about young British writers—when, told that he had won the Somerset Maugham Award (five hundred pounds to be spent on a three-month tour abroad) was reported to have said something to the effect of, "What a bore. It was bad enough travelling from Nottingham to London."

This insularity—broken down though it might seem to be by the works of young men who get sent to Bangkok by the British Council, or by a provincial university on an exchange basis to the Middle West, and for whom, to judge by the stream of definitive novels then published, the academic year is long enough to absorb the *ambiance* either of the ancient Orient or the new Occident—this insularity is as well to bear in mind when approaching any work of British creative writing offered to us today. As well, it is useful to recognize that any English boy or girl has the opportunity—indeed the encouragement— to become a writer these days. Given a ream of paper, a clutch of pencils, a room off the Fulham Road with a gas ring and a double bed, a weekly contribution from the National Assistance, a monthly check from Daddy in St. John's Wood, or a weekly wage from the Empire Catering Company—the lower slopes of Parnassus are available to anyone, and are frequently inhabited, so much so that it is often difficult to elbow your way through the crowd to see what the boys and girls in the middle and upper regions are doing.

Arriving in those regions on our hands and knees, dizzy from stray blows suffered from becoming transiently involved in punchups between our latter-day Tom Joneses, or in sessions of bodice-ripping and hair-pulling conducted by the black-eyed descendants of our old friend Moll Flanders, we find, not the *Pax Britannica,* but the even greater threat of a Samurai sword—said to be an excellent instrument for severing heads; and if we dodge this threat, and continue remembering our Bunyan, we find ourselves, in succession, in the civilized but tricksy maze designed by Mrs. Muriel Spark, then standing in exhausted admiration of the lofty spire of Mr. William Golding, until, emerging from the choking areas of art to the relatively soothing acres of artifice, we can enjoy the lower reaches of the regions inhabited by the Abominable Snowman (C. P. that is), the well-mannered man's James Bond—the head of our secret service, who makes out the checks Bond spends on liquor and women or on the marginal aspects of our modern technology. The soporifics offered by the new establishment to the new-deprived. By new-deprived, I mean *us*.

Having worked hard, and honorably, for his power, Snow is infinitely aware of the ordinary human weaknesses that lead us into bad habits, dishonest professions, and a kinky interest in gold paint. But the first chapter of *The Corridors of Power* is a perfect example of the post-1945 narrows into which the popular British novel has sailed. Snow, the old wizard, commands the objects of our envy and translates them into those of our joyous possession. In at last. What bliss. To share Lewis Eliot's success in the world of affairs assisted by all the loaded little asides that prove Snow knows and can teach us to distinguish a coming man from one suffering from some kind of serious interruption because he has been to the wrong grammar school—such a short, and not the least painful step from sharing, on a different, and yet not so different, level, James Bond's success with women.

This hunger *to* be, rather than not to be, to have and to hold and never to lose, never to give away again and yet not become—ever—less than cynical about one's possessions, is perhaps the whole point about the English today.

In the past, writers presented worlds which, attractive as many parts of them were, on the whole we shrank from, as it was intended we should, recognizing that these were visions of the one we lived in, and ought to do something about. Today we are more often shown worlds we don't *quite* recognize as our own, but are encouraged to aspire to—the product of someone else's in-knowledge or switched-on experience of sex, money, or power, but it is no good criticizing this development. We are all responsible for it because we are hungry for new experience—not for its own sake but for the sake of where this complex of corridors might lead. For we are still a practical people. As practical as children. As children we are capable still of recognizing the difference between our real world and our dream world. The possible danger lies in the moment when too many of us believe there is *no* difference, when we wake up believing we are Lord Snow's perennial hero, Lewis Eliot, and set out for the House of Commons thinking we are Agent 007 and go crazy looking for Pussy Galore, when we believe that writing is life, and life is artifice.

But, for the moment, why not, in our literature, the comic strip, the cardboard cut out, the parlor game, the sense of play, as well as the book which Alice found dull because there were no illustrations, but which her sister seemed to find so absorbing?

Perhaps the most revealing witness of the confusion of the last two decades in English letters is the cloud–cuckoo argument that went on about what are called "the Two Cultures": an argument that exacerbated the tempers of people who had never read any of the novels in dispute. For those of us who remained unmoved by this storm in a university teapot, answered by the faint tinkling of a Whitehall spoon, there has been no vacuum, no realization that there was a choice to be made or a bridge to be built between commitments to science and the humanities, no awareness that in a common humanity there ever could be more than one basic culture.

What we might have been aware of is the danger of our culture succumbing to the fragmentation of narrow definitions. Becoming, therefore, the culture of an intensely narrow age, masquerading as latitudinarian. Free and broad of speech, mean of heart. Radical in protestation, reactionary in performance. Active in thought, lazy in habit. Satirical in style, pedagogic in manner. Tolerant on the surface, violently disposed under-neath. A culture and an age of disenchantment with estab-lished processes, or disenchantment with the notion that any process should ever become established again. An uncharitable culture and a restive age, because our old reforming impulses bore fruits that turned out sour.

And this, perhaps, *is* our age and our culture, because by and large this is the age and culture our literature seems to reflect. The interesting thing is that it also reflects something else: vitality. The vitality of a people who are alive enough to know that they are not living, but pondering, seeking new def-initions of almost every aspect of human exchange. Tempers are short. Vulgarity is intense. The dangers are great. The pos-sibilities are enormous. This *is* our society. This *is* our litera-ture. By literature I mean any kind, every aspect, of writing. This may not be immediately clear to those of you who, with a kind of superior snob-modesty, make no claim to contribute to literature as such. Are there any such here? If so, I hope by the end of the week they will have changed their minds. Are there any here who say, with that undisciplined doglike look, "I only want to tell a story?" If so, perhaps by the end of the week they will be asking themselves *why* they want to tell one. "Let me quote from the OED again. "*Literature*. Noun. Literary culture. (Archaic). Literary production: The literary profession. Realm of letters—Writings of a country or period. The books treating of a subject. Printed matter."

At least on the broad basis of that minimal definition, "printed matter," we're all representative of our literature, the inheritors of our literary tradition. This puts us under certain obligations to it, and to each other. It isn't just a question of avoiding certain pitfalls—or the kind not altogether unknown at gatherings such as this—the kind that lead, say, crime writ-ers and romantic novelists to gather up the trains of their cloaks to avoid the contamination of one another, and poets to hold their noses in the air when passing a group of short story writers, who, for their part, stop talking if a playwright goes by. Neither is it just a question of encouraging the old to mix with the young, or of discouraging the young from segregating themselves from the old. It would of course be nice if these clannish instincts were temporarily smothered. But it is a question, above all, of being alive in the way that literature must always be alive—to the past, to the present, to the opportunities of the future.

Perhaps during the rest of the week, in the intervals between the sessions of detailed, specialized study, a thought might be held in the back of the mind for the larger context of the work we are doing, or hoping to do. If this proves to be possible, and if you find that it adds an extra dash of interest to your severely professional deliberations, then I shall be glad. Not just at the thought that you'll then be getting more for your money, nor just at the thought that your age, your experience, your success or relative failure, your particular interests suddenly assume a lesser importance than you imagine. I'll be glad because you'll then be getting more out of Swanwick, by putting just that bit more into it than you might have intended to. The seventeenth Summer School might then rank to an even greater extent than its sixteen predecessors as a microcosm of the fascinating, diverse, but vigorously alive society we have *all* created. And if this talk has left you feeling that nothing is sure, nothing is planned, nothing has yet been achieved of any lasting value, remember the old Chinese saying: It is better to travel than to arrive.

Thank you, and good luck.

MEET THE AUTHOR: MANCHESTER

◆

["Meet the Author: Manchester" is the text of a lunchtime lecture that Scott gave at the Manchester Library Theatre during National Book Week in Manchester on March 9, 1967. Coming less than a year after the publication of The Jewel in the Crown, *this occasion offered him the chance to let readers in the general public see the especially personable side of a private man who was also an author, and to enjoy some of his wit. This essay gives, in his own words, a sense of who Paul Scott was, why he became a full-time writer at age forty, what his writing habits were, and why he wrote about India. Along with "A Writer Takes Stock," included later in this collection of essays, and some paragraphs scattered through Scott's letters, this essay is one of the very few sources of biographical information about him.]*

Up until last week I was a bit wary about this morning's appointment. In the first place, I hoped there wasn't going to be a misunderstanding. In the past, my name on a program has, I believe, led some members of the audience to expect an illustrated lecture on nature reserves or polar exploration. Indeed, I entertain the gravest suspicion that a book of mine called *The Birds of Paradise* enjoyed a success not wholly due to what went on between the covers.

In the second place, I wondered whether the fact that people could shorten or change, or give up, their lunch hour to Meet an Author couldn't be seen as further evidence of the decline in our society of a serious sense of values, and that they should actually pay for the dubious entertainment offered proof that the affluent society was a disagreeable reality—that people had more money than was good for them, would do anything for a laugh, go anywhere to escape from the yawning chasm of too much leisure.

It wasn't as though there was a binge to go with it—one of those luncheons whose components you know in advance:

cream of mushroom soup

a sliver of luke-warm plaice with an
unidentifiable sauce

a half-cooked piece of chicken
swimming in transparent gravy

followed by *bombe surprise,* a cup of coffee brewed from pencil shavings, and one or two Captive Speakers to rumble in opposition to the uncertain flow of the digestive juices. There wasn't— so far as I knew—even a prize for the holder of a lucky ticket: a holiday for two on the Costa Brava, a Night Out with a Television Personality. There was nothing, except a handful of hopeful booksellers, you and me—and the terrible expanse of silence that had to be filled.

But then—on Saturday—my copy of *The Bookseller* arrived, and on page 1433 I read the following:

Sales Queues in Manchester

There were extraordinary scenes in Manchester on the opening day of the National Book Sale. W. H. Willshaw had hired a shop in a central position especially for the Sale, and the crush there became so great that the doors had to be closed. A *queue formed* and during the lunch-hour was never less than twenty people, in spite of the usual rain. Other retailers told Mr.John Prime, Willshaw's managing director, that they had not seen such queues since the war.

Well, of course, that explained everything. In Manchester you're all mad. You queue for books, and a community that queues for books is probably serious about Meeting an Author. Wariness gave way to respect—the respect one bibliomaniac must feel for a whole townful of them. I felt I couldn't get away with a few poorly timed jokes and a light-hearted survey of the contemporary scene. Of course, I didn't automatically assume that the books you'd been queuing for were all mine, but putting in a personal appearance—so hard on the heels of this public demonstration of wild enthusiasm for the Products of Authorship—I felt, as it were, both representative and under a personal obligation to account for myself. I felt that the generic title of these lectures should not be "Meet the Author," but "Meet the Reader." And a very special type of reader at that: The Manchester species—ruminative, but uncontrollable when roused.

I found myself, for no very clear reason, silently reciting the chorus of "The Ballad of East and West."

> Oh East is East, and West is West,
> and never the Twain shall meet,
> Till Earth and Sky stand presently
> at God's great Judgment Seat;
> But there is neither East nor West,
> Border, nor Breed, nor Birth,
> When two strong men stand face to face,
> tho they come from the ends of the earth!

The image didn't seem entirely satisfactory. But the feeling that it fit persisted. So I looked the poem up and found the line:

> They have looked each other between the eyes,
> *and there they found no fault.*

And that seemed more like it.

All the same, in fact more pertinently than ever, there was the question of what to talk about. Authors on the whole are not very interesting people. William Faulkner shunned publicity for that very reason, until he found himself the recipient of the Nobel Prize and, having to make a speech, said that his biography should be one sentence long: "He wrote the books and he died."

Admirable sentiment. Providing his books are read, no author could wish for a better memorial. Last summer I sat opposite a man in the tube who was reading a novel I'd just published, *The Jewel in the Crown.* He looked like a lawyer, a man of stolid virtues and solid worth. We both got out at Chancery Lane. It was a quiet part of the morning, there were few other passengers, and I was behind him on the escalator. Part of me wanted to tap him on the shoulder and ask: "Are you enjoying it?" But one has to be careful, especially on the underground. And there was the question of his reply. "Since you mention it—No." Or, "What's it got to do with you?" Improbable, surely, that he would turn to me with a look of beatitude and say, "Oh yes, I am! And surely? No—it can't be! But it is! My dear chap—the untold hours of pleasure."

So I did nothing. And what better answer could he have given me than the one he did, which was to continue reading as the escalator moved us upwards. Rather like poor Blanche Dubois in Tennessee Williams's play, *A Streetcar Named Desire,* authors depend a great deal for well-being and peace of mind on the unconscious courtesy of strangers.

It is a courtesy you pay me consciously this morning by

coming to listen. I must try to repay it, in the only way I know, by talking as objectively as possible about the author you've come to meet.

In the public mind there are various ideas of the literary gent. For instance, there is the Tortured Genius, wrestling with a neurotic and unpunctual muse, whose visitations are infrequent enough for him to fill the gaps with wild indulgence or hermit disappearance into a private life whose fascinating enormity will be revealed only after his death. Then there is the Bland Practitioner, who works his casual stint of three highly productive hours every morning, connecting himself to an apparently inexhaustible supply of inspiration, as if it were a sort of instant piped music of the kind you get in pubs and supermarkets, after which he will have a light luncheon and devote the rest of the day to being civilized.

Next there is the Switched-on Intellectual—a formidable figure—who belongs to committees, adds his signature to group letters to the *Times,* and whose attitude to the burning problems of the day is not only sought but enthusiastically volunteered. There is the Roaring Boy—and his counterpart, the Swinging Literary Gal—a whole contingent of them, all speaking for their generation, all potential candidates for any of the previously mentioned classifications. And behind all these images, a conveyed sense of privilege, perhaps—a sort of ghastly seriousness about the business of *being* a writer. An idea that being a writer involves far more than writing books. Indeed, that writing the books is a rather boring occasional chore, like having to put in a certain number of appearances in Dining Hall to qualify for residence.

When I consider these images, I find myself not fitting any one. Neither Tortured Genius, Bland Practitioner, Switched-on Intellectual, Roaring Boy—nor even Swinging Gal. Those are the negatives. The positives are unspectacular.

Age: Coming up to 47. Married, with two daughters, aged

twenty and nearly nineteen, respectively, the one interested in the production side of theater, the younger reading English and philosophy at York University. Background: Middle class. Hostages to fortune: wife, family, mortgage, overinsurance, and a four-door family sedan. Hobbies: Gardening. Occupation?

Well, for that, let me quote the words of the critic Miss Kathleen Nott, writing in a magazine called *Encounter.* "In a good sense, I believe," she wrote, "Mr. Scott is a professional novelist." She did not say what a bad sense was, but in any case I thought I detected a note of mild rebuke. It seemed to be in her mind that while my novels reached, from her point of view, a certain acceptable literary standard, since I had found no other visible means of support—wasn't employed for instance by the British Council, did not teach, seldom contributed to magazines, didn't write plays, poetry, biography, serious criticism as distinct from casual reviewing—these novels must be written, not from a deep compulsion, but from habit and financial necessity.

How true is that?

There must be some truth in it, I suppose, but I should hate to think that habit and financial necessity dictated either the type of book I write or the frequency and *speed* with which I write them. I like to think that into every book I write I put the utmost effort and allow it to dictate its own pace. However, years and experience bring about a change in your idea of effort and a change in pace.

In mid-career, a professional novelist—either in the good or bad sense—will have behind him a number of books the surface detail of which will seem totally strange to him. For instance, when preparing these notes, I picked up a copy of my first novel, long out of print, and read—just at random—the following passage:

The sergeant said, He'll get here in a minute.
Jim had no doubt that whoever he was he would.

Which is more than I can say for myself. I know who Jim is—the hero—but who would get where in a minute for what purpose, and why Jim was sure the sergeant, whoever the sergeant was, was forecasting accurately, escapes me utterly. Perhaps at the time the two sentences cost me a cup of coffee and two cigarettes before I was sure that Jim would react in this way. More likely, because this was a first book, I didn't stop to consider Jim's reaction at all. I just felt it, and had the sublime self-assurance to believe what I felt was right.

At the time it probably all seemed splendid and inevitable—reminiscent now of the approach of an even earlier, more distant, *unpublished* period, a period of work no doubt signed with a flourish, Paul Scott. Or Paul Mark Scott. I wonder what happened to him? What happened to the impatient and care-free youth who wrote a whole chapter of a novel between dinner and bedtime, a three-act play between Monday and Friday, composed a sonnet in the short time it took one morning to shave the hopeful fluff from chin and cheeks, and did not care who admired or scoffed at these brilliant sparks that seemed to fly so casually from the crater of his apparently volcanic talent?

Well I don't know what happened to him, but I know what happened to the apparently volcanic talent. It's probably best described as having diminished to the size of a single rather cold blue flame, not unlike the pilot light of a gas appliance—thin and steady, waiting for a supply of fuel from which it can create the likeness of an explosion.

And of course it hasn't really diminished to this. It was never anything else. It's just that in youth there seems to be such an endless supply of proper fuel, but when you really begin to practice you quickly learn that there's only one type of fuel suitable for your particular machine. Feed the wrong type into it and it won't work, or will sputter and cough and seize up. I could no more write a James Bond-type thriller than I could fly unassisted to the moon.

But why do I write at all? To supply a demand? Because I

can't do anything else? Because it satisfies my ego—gives me a feeling of power? Or because it helps me to escape from reality? Frees me from other *tedious* obligations? I THINK THE *JUST* ANSWER TO ALL THOSE QUESTIONS IS: *NO*.

And that the only true answer is that I write because I have a natural aptitude for it, a sense of vocation. Why I have the aptitude is a mystery. I suppose it's something to do with the *genes*, with the nature of an individual sensibility. One of the earliest signs of the so-called creative instinct in childhood is self-absorption—the feeling that you are somehow separate from your environment and can't identify with it really satisfactorily—plus the feeling that this inability, far from being *wrong*, ought to be cultivated. It shows up in very ordinary things—for instance, I was a gifted sprinter and high-jumper, but not a good team man. Give me a tape and two hundred twenty yards of space between me and it, and other people to outdistance, and I was there. Give me a bat and instructions to stay in and hold my end up, and what happened? A couple of sweeps to leg—showy in intent, clumsy in fact—and that was it. Only alone in the deep field could I sufficiently identify with a game involving others to come out of my grass-scented reverie, to watch a spherical object mysteriously approaching from the boundless blue, see it as mine, get beneath it, catch and hold it to my breast in a paroxysm of selfish joy. The applause from the pavilion was always gratifying but wasn't the object of the exercise.

This self-absorption is a form of curiosity, and after a while when it's worked itself out, a different kind of curiosity takes its place and is just as sharp—a curiosity in *other* people. There is something common to both forms: that is the curiosity in the environment—in the physical surroundings. This doesn't change, and I suppose the child who is going to be a writer is more curious about his surroundings than the child who wants to be—and feels—part of them. This is a post-Freudian age, and I'm not talking about emotional security and insecurity. I think it's true to say that in the absence of a real one, the creative child will invent his own unhappy childhood. He is a natural rearranger. A natural rejector.

The older I get, the less I believe in the theory that our environment makes us what we are—and the more I believe in the influence of the mysterious genes.

But whatever way you look at it, it all added up to the fact that I had the aptitude—felt that I had the aptitude to invent, rearrange, impose a different kind of order on reality by telling stories that would reflect my vision of it—and proved it by writing; and doing that, perhaps, a shade better than I did anything else.

The next question to be answered is why and when I became a *professional* writer—in my sense of the word. Which is to say, full-time. I didn't become a full-time writer until the age of forty. I became one then for several reasons. Not because I thought I was going to make more money that way than any other. That seemed highly debatable. But in writing four or five novels—as I had done, while doing another, full-time job—I made the remarkable discovery that the more novels you write the more difficult they become. This is when you first begin to recognize that the volcanic fire is really a cold small steady blue flame. And then there was this other reason. I have learned to hate half-heartedness in anything. I have this old-fashioned notion that if a thing's worth doing, it's worth trying to do well. It seemed to me it was a question of making a choice between writing full-time, or gradually not writing at all. And *that* I thought of as insupportable.

In the last *seven* years, then, I have sat down at my desk, more or less every day, and I've produced a total of four novels, amounting in all, I suppose, to half-a-million words. And included in those seven years—but not in the total number of words—there's the work in progress, which has occupied me now getting on for eighteen months.

Readers, I'm told, are interested in individual working

methods, so perhaps I'll add a footnote that, following the advice of—Who was it? Henry James? It's bound to be. It's usually Henry James—I keep my daily appointment with the Muse, whether or no she turns up.

Over a period variations appear in the schedule, but by and large you can say that I work from nine o'clock until one o'clock; have lunch between one and two; between two and four have some fresh air, either by walking or gardening; have tea; and return for an evening stint of perhaps two and a half hours between five and seven-thirty.

The work produced, day by day, is very uneven. And the percentage of wastage is pretty high. Of the manuscript of the work in progress I have at home at the moment—say four inches thick—one-and-a-half inches represents what has already been discarded.

There comes a moment in every book when you know you are committed to it. There are times when you hate it. When you think it's defeated you. When the book in itself has, as it were, *gone out* and only this pilot light—your knowledge that you are committed to it with every part of your writing nature—continues to burn. This is what is known as writer's mental or psychological block.

It's then a question of perseverance. Of not giving up hope. Of being prepared to cut back, rethink. A lot of the difficulties in writing a book turn out to have been due to an unhappy marriage between form and content. Writers whose content varies little from book to book will seldom have any trouble with form. By content I don't mean just subject matter, but your approach to it.

A restless writer—and I think I am one—will always be varying his approach to his subject matter, varying his content (still rejecting and rearranging you note), and having difficulty, as a consequence, with form.

I spoke some while ago about what I called the ghastly seriousness that sometimes surrounds the public image of the writer and the writer's image of himself. I'm not contradicting myself if I now describe myself as a serious writer. You can write books seriously without taking your profession in itself as serious—in the sense of it being essential and superior. In its public aspect, it has some very comic sides. And all books are fun when you really think about it. Any human experience is *fun*, and a book *is* an experiment, an attempt to make something new out of familiar material.

There are, I should say, two main kinds of serious writer. There is the kind who has an intense curiosity in the immediate present, in the world around him, in what—as it were—*is going on*. This is the kind of serious writer who will tend not to have trouble with form. He has something to say about the society immediately under our noses, and more likely than not will have no difficulty about saying it in the most straightforward manner.

I wouldn't put myself in that category. Not because I don't also have an intense curiosity and interest in the society I actually live in. I do. But because my kind of curiosity is a comparative one.

I think this suggests that I have a sort of puritan instinct, a hatred of *waste*. A sense that the present should always be seen in relation to the past and to the future.

Years and years ago, when I first read some of the essays of the American writer Emerson, as a youth, his essay on history must have made some impact on me, but I was struck by it forcibly, quite recently, when picking up my daughter's copy and glancing at it, to read these opening words:

> There is one mind common to all individual men. Every man is an inlet to the same and to all of the same. He that is once admitted to the right of reason is made a freeman of the whole estate. What Plato has thought, he may think; what a saint has felt, he may feel; what at any time has befallen any man, he can understand.

Of the works of this mind, history is the record. Its genius is illustrated by the entire series of days. Man is explicable by nothing less than all his history. Without hurry, without rest, the human spirit goes forth from the beginning to embody every faculty, every thought, every emotion, which belongs to it, in appropriate events. But always the thought is prior to the fact; all the facts of history pre-exist in the mind as laws. . . .

I was struck by this because it explained so much of what I have come to feel as an individual. On the prosaic level of application it also explains why the characters in my novels usually have—demonstrably—personal histories whose *weight* they feel along with the weight of their presents and their expectations for the future.

It also explains my passion for form—which is another word for wholeness, not just tidiness—and the difficulties I have matching form to content, because this sense of wholeness in life—that is to say, wholeness in the subject matter of my books—is a difficult thing to sustain under the weight of so much apparent evidence that this is an age which, on the surface, seems devoted to the concept of built-in obsolescence and to be suffering from the self-inflicted wound of the notion that the past, having been a conspicuous failure—if life is to be seen as the pursuit of reason and the pursuit of happiness—is better mocked than appraised, better forgotten than remembered.

Finally it explains why, as a writer, twenty years after India gained her independence, I nevertheless feel that in writing about those last days of the British I'm writing about things that still have a bearing on our society. Obviously I must have a reason for writing about India, or rather about the British in India, because looked at simply as a subject, it would seem to be one of the most foolhardy to choose. In the first place, there are the British people themselves—who, even while they *had* India, showed very little interest or curiosity in it. And in the second place, of course, there is E. M. Forster. And no writer about

India now can fail to have his attention drawn by critics to the fact that he has been preceded. For the British, on the whole, there have been three Indias. Kipling's, Forster's, and currently the comic India as conveyed by the impersonations of Mr. Peter Sellers.

If I had never written a book about India, no critic, I think, would have thought to compare my work in any way with that of Forster. Since it is easy to detect which of them mean it as a compliment and which as a dressing-down, it doesn't worry me overmuch and it reminds me—of course, rather usefully— that, as a subject, the British in India were dealt with—from many other people's points of view—superbly and for all time in 1924.

I say usefully, because this knowledge can only properly goad me to an extreme of self-criticism and self-interrogation. It helps me to clarify—to explain to myself— my own continuing compulsive interest.

India, to me, was the scene of a remarkable and far-reaching event. I see it as the place where the British came to the end of themselves as they were. It was, even more than England was, the scene of the victory of liberal humanism over dying paternal imperialism.

This was a fact of history—1947, to be precise—but, as Emerson said, "All the facts of history pre-exist in the mind as laws." And by the time the facts occur, the laws—that is to say the moral laws—which create the historical events are already old and tired, conscious of their own failings, their own built-in weaknesses and defects.

The special fascination that India has for me is the almost tragic atmosphere I see as attaching to it then—and indeed still— as the mausoleum containing the remains of the last two great senses of public duty we had as a people. I mean of course the sense of duty that was part and parcel of having an empire, and the sense of duty so many of us felt, that to get rid of it was the liberal human thing to do.

Getting rid of India involved the lives, then, of four-hundred million people. They say two-hundred thousand of them died by each others' hands. Returning to the scene in fiction isn't due to nostalgia, or to guilt. I return to it because to me the death and interment of liberal humanism is still a living issue in the terms meant by my sort of novelist and my sort of reader.

By liberal humanism I mean, broadly, the human consciousness of human dignity that began with the Renaissance and came to an end in the form we knew it in the Second World War and its aftermath. Our imperialism was as much an expression of it as our reforming zeal. We are still, quite properly, bent on reforms, but we carry them through, I think, by the power of momentum—dispassionately, a bit cynically—for the sake of a kind of peace of mind. But the mind is detached. It is practical rather than inspired. An act to legalize abortion has nothing to do with a concept of the dignity of unmarried mothers, nor one to legalize affairs between consenting adults with the dignity of queers. The dignity would be a human dignity, and our notions of that have faded. We're no longer certain what a human being is. Perhaps in our recognition of that fact is the seed of a new dignity to be developed—the acts of future history exist now in our mind as laws. On the first page of *The Jewel in the Crown* I spoke of what I call the moral continuum of human affairs. Perhaps consciousness of its existence is also a kind of dignity. I hope so. Above all I hope that I've been able to portray it—in some small way—in the stories I've written about things that never happened, and yet are happening all the time.

Finally I must thank the sponsors who invited me here—my publishers who escorted me up here by the First Class—and all of you who have turned out and turned up—refreshed, presumably, rather than jaded by your terrific exertions in the National Book Sale. Thank you.

METHOD: THE
MYSTERY AND THE
MECHANICS

◆

*["Method: The Mystery and the Mechanics" is the closing address
to the participants of the Writers' Summer School, Swanwick, 1967—
the third of the four lectures Scott gave there over a fifteen-year
period. In this lecture, he explores generally the relation between
imagination and the act of writing, a theme which appears again in
"Imagination in the Novel" (1961) and the Stamford Grammar
School lecture (1975), both of which are printed in this collection.
Furthermore, he makes extended comments about composing* The
Jewel in the Crown. *After describing the image at the core of his
novel, Scott then discusses how history, personal experience, and
imagination came together in his own creative process—his personal
"method."]*

The subtitle of this talk on method is "the Mystery and the
Mechanics"—which does not mean a detective story about the
murder of a garage hand. The method I have in mind is my
own personal method, for my own kind of novels. When talking to this school in the past, I've always been conscious of the
dangers of talking about *how* it is done, because you can only
talk about how *you* do it—and that, apart from being dangerous, is far from easy.

But tonight I want to attempt the difficult thing, the dangerous thing. Tomorrow—unless we're lucky enough to be off

on holiday somewhere—we all go back home, and for a writer, going back home means back to the pen, pencil, and type-writer—and the blank, implacable sheet of white paper.

And when you think of that, you may have a sinking feel-ing in the heart. I know *I* do, every morning when I go upstairs and into the study. I envy those people who can't wait to get at it, whose fingers positively itch. I used to be like that too, of course, so perhaps what I really envy is their youth if they are young, or their happy-go-luckiness if they are not.

But I see no reason why a writer shouldn't suffer from the same nervous tension, the almost-hatred of what he is about to try and do, that the actor feels waiting in the wings. The im-portant thing is to know that you *can* do it.

What you must guard against is excessive self-confidence. It is as bad for your work as lack of confidence. Every time you put a word on paper you are taking a risk—much the same sort of risk that a painter takes when he makes a brushmark on his canvas. Well, he can paint it over, and you can rub your word out. But that is a risk, and the word you substitute is another risk.

You are risking the work you have in your mind every time you write a word of it. The words are tremendously important. They are not precious, though. Every word you write is *poten-tially* expendable, potentially a *misfit*. Be prepared to recognize that and accept it, be prepared to discard words and find others, and go on discarding and finding until something tells you that, "Yes—This is what was in my mind. Now it is on paper and is as close as I can get."

The words are part of the mechanics. What is in your mind is part of the mystery. Sometimes the words, when written, can be seen to have created little mysteries of their own. When you feel that happening, then you know that things *are* working right, because a proper balance exists between the mystery and the mechanics. The work will convey this to a reader. He will be conscious of an air of stability, of toughness, of reality; but he will also sense the presence of something indefinable. A quality, if you like, of magic. That is, in fact, what I mean by the mystery. It is a quality of mind. It is very precious. It is part of your writer's tone of voice.

I was asked once by someone in this school to say what style was and how it could be acquired. I said that style was the individual tone of voice, and could not be taught. A singer can be trained to do things like breathe correctly and phrase felicitously. He can be taught how to get the best out of his voice, but the voice itself is what he begins and ends with. So it is with the writer. His mind is his voice, and a mind is a more difficult thing to train. It cannot, in fact, be trained except by the person to whom it belongs. The most that a teacher can do is try to remind that person, that writer, that he does have a mind, and that whatever he learns about the technique of writing will do no more than improve the *surface* of his work.

That's not quite true. It *will* improve the surface, but that will also expose the comparative strength or weakness of his individual voice—the thing that gives a work or deprives a work of what we call depth. Technique is a trap. The more you acquire—and you must acquire it—the more you will be exposed. It is useless to learn a technique and then arbitrarily adopt it for your own work. It is best to *feel* for the work that is in your mind, the work only you can write because no one else has a mind just like yours, and then to slave diligently at putting it on paper in such a way that other people can see what you have seen in the way you have seen it. The way you put it will be *your* method, *your* technique. It will expose you, but it will be a compound of *your* mystery and *your* mechanics.

Am I harping too much on that word mystery? I do so intentionally, as a corrective to two general ideas that can all too easily run away with people at a gathering of writers or would-be writers such as this. The first of these general ideas is that all you have to do is learn a few rules and regulations, and you can become a good writer. The second idea is that successful

73

writers are in possession of some special secret that they won't, under any circumstances, divulge.

Neither idea has any foundation in fact. There are no rules and regulations the learning of which will *ensure* success. There is no closely guarded secret. The plain fact of the matter is that as writers we are not born equal. Our gifts are diverse, and our rewards are as diverse as our gifts. It would be superhuman of us not sometimes to envy this man's gift or that man's reward. But that won't help us tomorrow, say, when we climb the stairs, enter the study, and face the blank white paper.

What will?

Presumably people come to this school to get help so that they go back to the blank white paper feeling they know a bit more. What they will know is a bit more about how other people do it, how other people fill the page. But they will also, I hope, have been encouraged. I have always felt that the main purpose of the Writers' Summer School is to give encouragement. Is it an encouragement if I assure you that no one in this room will have a *more* difficult job to start covering that sheet of white paper than the writer standing at this lectern in what appears to be a place of temporary superiority?

It is meant to be an encouragement, and it is no means lightly meant.

Well, let us assume that during this past week you have been encouraged and are going home knowing a bit more about how other people do it. Now I've got to try and tell you how *I* do it, how I write my novels. It may or may not help you to write yours!

A novel is a sequence of images. In sequence these images tell a story. Its purpose is not to *tell* you but to *show* you. Creative writing is showing, not telling. The words used to convey the images and the act of juxtaposing the images in a certain way are the mechanics of the novel. But the images are what matter. They are the novel's raw material. Images are what we are really working with, and they are infinitely complex.

Constructing a novel—telling a tale, for me at any rate—is

not a business of thinking of a story, arranging it in a certain order, and then finding images to fit it. The images comes first. I may have a general notion of wanting to write a book about a certain time, or place, but unless the general notion is given the impetus of an image that seems to be connected, the notion never gets off the ground.

Well, there is a problem there, because as writers, our minds teem with images. We have unending stocks of these private little mysteries, and it is all too easy to think of a story, a situation, and come up with an adequate supply of mental pictures to illustrate it. I call that automatic writing. I don't decry it. It can be very effective. But it isn't my way, and in automatic writing of this kind you seldom feel, as a reader, that there is much underneath. The images conveyed are flat, two-dimensional. In fitting an image to a situation, the image lacks density, it has little ability to stand on its own. It has no inner mystery. *The situation, somehow, must be made to rise out of the image.*

You need, to begin with, a strong central image that yields a strong situation, or series of situations. By strong I don't necessarily mean strongly dramatic. I mean strong in the sense of tenacious, one that won't let you off the hook. Almost every one of your waking hours is spent considering it, exploring it. You can carry on a conversation and still be thinking of it— although you do tend to lose your awareness of the lapse of real time. When in the grip of this kind of image, my wife may say to me over the breakfast table, "Darling, is it raining?" Two seconds later—but actually two minutes—after she has been to the window, looked out and seen for herself that it is, I will probably say, "No, I don't think so." This is called absence of mind. But absent is exactly what the mind is not. At least it isn't absent from the place where its duty is to be—in the embryo book, wallowing through all the sticky, unmapped, unexplored regions of this extraordinary picture that so far has not been fully transformed into a situation.

Such a picture is a combination of our experience, imagination, knowledge and creative impulse. In this combination is to be found our personal mystery. We should be content to leave it to others to elucidate or interpret that mystery—if they can—in any terms they wish, although there is a critical movement nowadays against interpretation, a growing recognition of the fact that, analyze and interpret how you will, a novel that has any serious claim to be a work of art will always—in its essence—defy the attempt to render it down to its chemical ingredients. The novelist will do well to reserve, in his approach to the mechanical side of his craft, a sense of the mysterious reality of the essence he is dealing with—that aspect of it which the mechanics are incapable of controlling, that aspect which will, in fact, dictate the form the mechanics take if they are to do their job of presenting the image to others, as it has been seen and felt by the writer.

There are stresses and strains in the construction of a novel that we ignore at our peril. But the awful thing is that, unlike in bridge building, there are no actual laws of science to learn and apply. The image requires its own laws—and it is your job to find them. In the end you have to rely on instinct, a feeling for what will work, page for page, chapter for chapter, part for part.

Let me now attempt to exemplify some of these general remarks by discussing some actual writing problems, as I have encountered them. Since it is freshest in my memory, I'll deal with the last novel I published, a book called *The Jewel in the Crown*.

On the face of it, *The Jewel in the Crown* is about an English girl called Daphne Manners who falls in love with an anglicized Indian called Hari Kumar. In the opening stages of the Indian rebellion of 1942, Miss Manners is criminally assaulted by a gang of hooligans. The district superintendent of police promptly arrests Hari Kumar and five other boys of a similar type whom he finds drinking illicit liquor in a hut not far from the scene of the crime. They are, as a matter of fact, innocent, and the

Indians are convinced of that. Rumors of their torture and defilement add fuel to the fire of the riots that bring the Indian population and the British raj into a violent confrontation. These riots are widespread throughout the country. Their cause is political.

Here is a blend of fact and fiction. The riots are real. The historical and political scene is factual. The dramatic situation of the criminal assault, the arrests, the treatment of the prisoners, is imaginary, but it is based very broadly on fact.

In 1919 in Amritsar, at the onset of some earlier troubles in the Punjab, an Englishwoman—a mission school superintendent—was dragged off her bicycle by a gang of hooligans and beaten up. Six men were arrested at random. The lane in which the assault took place was sealed off by orders of one Brigadier General Dyer, a triangle was erected in the lane, and the six men who had been arrested were brought there from jail and whipped for what was called an infringement of prison regulations. Thereafter, any Indian who lived in the lane was made to crawl on his hands and knees along it to get to his front door.

Presently there occurred the affair of the shooting by the Gurkha troops, led by General Dyer, of a crowd of unarmed Indian civilians in an enclosed space called the Jallianwallah Bagh. The crowd had collected there in defiance of Dyer's orders prohibiting public meetings. They were not, however, warned to disperse but simply fired on. Women and children were among those killed. There was no way out of the Jallianwallah Bagh except over the walls. The troops were blocking the only exit.

This revolting episode has, as you may imagine, never been forgotten in India. The riots in the Punjab in 1919 were sparked off by the passing of what was called the Rowlatt Acts—a measure passed by the British government to extend into peacetime certain wartime measures taken to protect the realm. The Acts included the right to imprison without trial. It was an extraordinary thing to do, considering the aid given the British by Indians of all kinds during the Great War. In 1917, dominion status for India had been formally declared by the British as their intention. It seemed like a reward for Indian cooperation in the war effort. At this period, Mr. Gandhi was urging young Indians in London to support the war effort. The Congress party was lined up in cooperation too. But the behavior of the British government after the war, in taking these further repressive measures—which the Indians saw as a crude ruse to prohibit free speech—alienated Gandhi, the Congress party, and Indians in general. Hence the riots in the Punjab. Hence General Dyer and Jallianwallah Bagh.

At the time, the British in India hailed Dyer as a savior, a man who had nipped the revolution in the bud with a military version of gunboat diplomacy. At home, however—and when all was said and done, India was ruled by us, over here, through the House of Commons—we were alarmed at this mid-Victorian attitude persisting on into the post-Great War decade. Dyer was eventually had up on the carpet, and, quite properly, retired. He was ill from a disease of the brain which later killed him. The memsahibs of India collected twenty-six thousand pounds to help keep the wolf from the old general's door. Here we have an interesting human and political situation. History is often made by ill people. But mostly the story illustrates the fact that individual human action is subject to the pressure exerted by a collective conscience. It is this collective conscience that gives history its forward impetus, what I call its moral drift.

Now all these things were in my mind before I began to formulate the images that go to make up the work I called *The Jewel in the Crown*. I said a short while ago that fictional images are a combination of the writer's experience, imagination, knowledge, and creative impulse. Those things I have just outlined come under the heading of knowledge. By knowledge I don't just mean the assimilation of facts, but that assimilation plus one's attitude to them. The facts I have outlined exist in

78

a state of reality. They happened. I interpret them one way, you may interpret them in another way. Your knowledge as a writer, therefore, is probably quite different from mine. But my knowledge is part of my tone of voice. I must be aware of this. I must be constantly on the alert for the weaknesses in my interpretation of facts, which means I must try to see things, in this case, from Dyer's point of view, from the point of view of the ladies who collected twenty-six thousand pounds, and from the point of view of the unfortunate men and women and children whose sufferings roused them emotionally, perhaps, to take an intensely narrow and personal view, which in turn led them to take unjust and unworthy actions themselves. And when I've done all that, I must still come out with a firm opinion. Nothing is worse for a novel than for the novelist to see all sides of a question and fail to support one. You must commit yourself. Submit yourself to an inquisition, but, at its close, commit yourself. Stick your neck out. Your novel will then say something.

I said that certain things were in my mind before I began to formulate the images of *The Jewel in the Crown*, and I also said that broadly *The Jewel in the Crown* was about this girl Daphne Manners, in love with an Indian and being criminally assaulted. Where does she come from? From history? No. As a result of my having decided to write a novel about the Indian rebellion of 1942, and having worked out a formula to provide it with some spicy love interest and a spot of rape? No. I suppose you could have done it that way round, but a novel is about people, and until you have got the people you haven't, in my opinion, got the novel, because you don't know what these particular, these individual, living, human beings are, or what they are capable of. They can be pure figments of the imagination, or so distantly removed from real people you have briefly met as to rank as totally anonymous. They can be more closely related to real people you have a clear recollection of—people you have met and after a while said of them, "How

79

extraordinarily interesting." After which you tuck them away in the warm storage of your imagination. But whatever their origin, they must be sat near, thought of, watched. You expose them to the pressures of the world as you know it. They create pressures of their own, and respond to other pressures in an increasingly fascinating way. In other words, a kind of plot is forming around them. The plot is implicit in the image of them, in the images of them in situations.

In 1964 I went back to India, which has been my background for several books. This return visit was undertaken not for a specific purpose, but just to look, to find out whether the place still excited me. I had no novel in my mind. I met a number of interesting people. I stayed in cities, and for ten days in somewhat primitive conditions in a village. By primitive, I mean there was no formal arrangement for what polite people call one's morning duties, but I call going to the loo. It was a comic, fascinating, highly emotional experience, and taught me a lot about the Europeans' fear of black countries. It was a severe strain on my civilized liberal instincts. Towards the end of my stay I found myself shouting. Lizards popped out of my dressing-gown pocket. The daughter of the house washed my feet every time I entered the compound of the hut. The smell of breakfast cooked in clarified butter turned my stomach. Three or four times a day I was forced to walk, water jug in hand because toilet paper would have offended the sensibilities of my hosts, to that distant bourn of an open field from which I felt this traveler one day would certainly not return. I accompanied my host in the dark to a village where illicit liquor was distilled, because my gin had run out. I attended a cockfight. I did puja to the Lord Venkateswara—a manifestation of Vishnu the Preserver—in the local temple, and drank during the course of it what, from its bitter taste, I suspected to be cow's urine. I was made to eat alone. I was watched everywhere. I slept under the stars, nudged awake by restless, warm-breathed cattle. I was shaved each morning without soap—my soap might have been made, they thought, from the fat of a dead animal. The barber shaved my face with a cutthroat and water—forehead, cheeks, chin, eyelids. I smiled and was in terror of being blinded by a slip of his hand. While I was shaved, a group of men sat and watched the extraordinary sight of a white man getting rid of his bristles. One felt like a cross between Sanders of the River and the King of Siam. Sometimes a bus passed through that village, and sometimes my host took me for a ride in it. A chair would be brought out of the house and placed by the roadside, and I would be made to sit on it. To wait at a bus stop on a kitchen chair gives you a curious sense of your own unlikelihood.

So extraordinary was this experience that even while I was there in the village I began to make notes for what I thought of as a short novel. I even had a title for it, *The Mango Rain*. But it never came to anything. Why? Because there was no image, no image except that of myself in this situation. I returned to the fleshpots of Hyderabad, Madras, and Calcutta. What had happened really was that I had added to my knowledge—not just of the customs, the manners, and the artifacts of an alien culture—*but of the terrible dependence we have on our own familiar way of doing things if we are to spare thought and expend kindness on people apparently different from ourselves.* I understood better, therefore, the physical and emotional impulses that had always prompted the British in India to sequester themselves in clubs and messes and forts, to preserve, sometimes to the point of absurdity, their own English middle-class way of life. It was a simple-enough lesson. One could learn it from books. It is better for a writer to learn lessons from life.

For the rest of my stay in India, and well beyond it, I was consciously puzzling over this short novel that I called *The Mango Rain*. The title was vaguely symbolic. I wasn't quite sure what of. But in the south there is an out-of-season rain which comes in time to ripen the mangos. It is a ripener of fruit and a refresher of spirits. The fruit I had in mind was human love, the kind that crosses the barrier between castes and creeds, black and white. It was very hot in that village. We needed rain. I had needed it particularly. But there was no rain and no novel. I couldn't detach myself from my experience and my knowledge sufficiently far to give my imagination and my creative impulse a clear field. The images don't seem to come until you stand some way back from what might be their source.

What is interesting is that I passed my eventual novel by in Calcutta without realizing it. There was a girl there, and an anglicized Indian. They were having an affair, so it was said. No one cares much these days, especially in Calcutta, about that sort of thing. It was simply part of the scene, which perhaps explains why I passed it by. Besides which, in themselves, they weren't awfully interesting people.

My image came—as images always do, apparently by chance, unexpectedly—in the dark of a restless, sleepless night. Vaguely, one can trace the antecedents: the trauma of the Indian village experiences, the desire to get away, to run, the knowledge of the dangers that exist when you attempt to cross bridges, the whole feeling of the British in India, and the feeling of India itself—a vast, flat territory, strangely forbidding, somehow incalculable, ugly, beautiful. And there she was, my prime mystery, a girl in the dark, running, exhausted, hurt in some way, yet strangely of good heart—tough, resilient, her face and figure a sense rather than an observed condition. But she runs.

From what? To where?

If you turn to the first page of *The Jewel in the Crown*, you will find this image conveyed as exactly as it was possible to convey it:

The first paragraph reads:

Imagine then, a flat landscape, dark for the moment, but even so conveying to a girl running in the still deeper shadow cast by the wall of the Bibighar Gardens an idea of immensity, of distance, such as years before Miss Crane had been conscious of, standing where a lane ended and cultivation began.

It was not the first paragraph written. Between the originating image and its pinning down to the page, there is often a terrible gap of time and changing circumstance. If it is a good hard image it will stand. Nothing will erode it. But it is extremely difficult to coordinate it with all the sequences of images it gives birth to.

You will note, for instance, that in the first paragraph there is an image of the girl running, and a piece of unconnected, apparently unconnected, information: "an idea of immensity, of distance, such as years before Miss Crane had been conscious of, standing where a lane ended and cultivation began."

Clearly the running girl and Miss Crane are not the same person. Clearly the reference to the wall in the Bibighar Gardens, which fixes a locality, is not a part of the original image. Images never have names, exact locations. "Such as years before Miss Crane had been conscious of"—Images do not have exact time schedules. Names, locations, time schedules, plot references—these are what the images *create*. In the original image are the seeds of all of your novel. See your image, feel it, work it out in all its complexity to the best of your ability, and then try to put it all on the page. There is a different kind of mystery here. If you see clearly—I mean *really* see, if you feel strongly—I mean *really* feel, then however poor your mechanical ability, however sparse your techniques, somehow it will come through. Writing is not observation, it is feeling. You can observe accurately until kingdom come and transfer your observation into the acutest prose, and unless you feel what you observe it can still be as dead as a doornail.

As a creative writer you are not in the world to go round recording facts that everyone is perfectly capable of seeing or finding out for himself. You are in it to convey your individual response to the world we collectively inhabit and to facts we collectively know or are capable of knowing.

The images are your response. That is why I work from them, and from them alone. If you don't know in your bones what I mean by an image, you are not a creative writer.

Well, again I go back, to the image of the girl running. Once I had got it, received it if you like, although naturally I gave it to myself, I could treat it as a mine whose veins could be explored and exploited. Sometimes during the course of exploration an image peters out, as a mineral vein in a rock can peter out. Such images are totally expendable, and you expend them quickly enough. Never think of that as wasted time. Never be afraid *not* to write. Thinking is more important. I have found it useful, as I get older—and less confident—to consider the actual act of writing as a necessary hazard of my profession—the supreme bore, not unlike paying the income tax. One would give almost anything not to have to. How much better if you could become a sort of piped music, if readers could plug in to you and receive the images direct, paying you a bob a time—which is more than we shall ever get from the public libraries, or now, it seems, from what we call the undeveloped countries.

The image of the girl running didn't peter out—the veins of possible exploration became intensely complex. When you feel this happening you are at the heart of your mystery. Extracting the ore is the mechanical side of the operation, and to extract it you stand away from the image and subject it to a kind of bombardment, as if you're trying to split an atom. You bombard it with your knowledge, your experience, and your imagination, your creative impulse. If you're lucky you have a beautiful explosion.

With knowledge, experience, imagination, and creative impulse, I bombarded the image of the girl running. I had a beautiful explosion. But that, of course, was where the real work began—trying to convey that feeling of power and inevitability to others.

Bombarding the image with experience, the girl I'd met briefly in Calcutta came back to mind. Momentarily I saw *that* girl

84

running. Alas, she was a big, husky, not awfully attractive girl. My imagination fined her down, but at the point where the resilience of the girl in the image matched that of the girl in Calcutta, the fining-down process stopped, and Daphne Manners was born as tall, gangling, rather awkward. She was invested at once with a tendency to knock things over, and the running in darkness suggested shortness of sight and spectacles which she was too vain to wear. Experience also connected her to that anglicized Indian the girl in Calcutta had been in love with. So Daphne, too, had an anglicized Indian lover, but in real life he had been short and squat, and frankly one wondered how they managed. They belonged to farce or comedy, but my image had an air of tragedy about it. Fining the girl down, one heightened the boy into the physical likeness of someone who looked more like a man I met in Madras, someone who was, one felt, much more the kind of man the girl running in the dark would be attracted to. And there, experience and imagination temporarily stopped short, but the girl in the image now had physical attributes and the outline of an emotional history.

But from what was she running?

At this point you usually transfer the image into the context of your knowledge—which I've already described as what you *know* plus your attitude to it. You bombard the image with facts, and wait for them to stick. In this way the image takes on historical attributes. It becomes placed in time and circumstance. That English girl in Calcutta in 1964—nothing could ever have made her run—not there, not then. The girl in the image was running, you might say, from that village I stayed at. The village that had already been translated in my mind into a symbolic experience of a confrontation between East and West.

The last great confrontation between East and West in India was in 1942. At the end of 1941, and the beginning of 1942, the Japanese conquest of Malaya and Burma had brought the war right to India's doorstep. No one could blame the British for dismissing as highly irrelevant the claims of the Indian nationalists for self-government. No one could blame the Indians for thinking, "Well, here we go again, the British ask us to cooperate and promise all kinds of things for when the war is won. But what happened last time? The Rowlatt Acts, the massacre in the Jallianwallah Bagh. So why should we believe that after *this* war things will be any different?" There was, too, in the minds of many of Gandhi's followers, this rather curious and to us naïve idea that if the British left India, the Japanese wouldn't invade her. Were they not all Orientals? Men like Nehru saw the absurdity of this reasoning, but such men were unable to stand against the wave of deep anti-British feeling which swept India in 1942.

In March of that year, Stafford Cripps went out to discuss the situation with Indian leaders. The Cripps mission was bound to fail. He had nothing to offer except a plan for measures of self-government after the war. The plan was thrown out. Retrospectively, it is easy to say that the courageous and sensible thing would have been to co-opt the Indians into the war effort by bringing men like Nehru into the government. But when you are fighting for your lives, as the British expected to do in India in 1942, you do not relax control—you tighten it, and hope that everybody will see that really that is for the best for all concerned. The Indian Congress did not see it as for the best. The committee met and began to hammer out a policy—Gandhi's policy. Well, it was madness, but there was something magnificent about it too. It was a declaration of war on the British—nonviolent war—an ultimatum that unless self-government was granted immediately, the Congress would lead the nation in a mass civil disobedience that would make India untenable as a military base. The railways would stop, the docks would close, the war factories would come to a standstill. That was the resolution. On August 8th, the All-India Congress Committee adopted the resolution in Bombay. And at four A.M.

on the morning of August 9th, the British began to arrest every leading congressman in the country—quietly, without fuss. They just locked them all up, in the belief that if the leaders were in jail the people would continue docile. They didn't. On August 10th, almost throughout the country, the people rose in an attempt to put into operation the plans their now-jailed leaders had intended. It was a massive, dangerous enterprise, and it was in effect the last such confrontation in British–Indian history. Among the British colony there was a belief that something on the lines of a new Indian Mutiny was about to take place. It was stamped out with the determination you would expect of a people who had no time or patience for such irrelevancies. Well—against such a background, yes, there might be a girl, a white girl, running in the darkness. I had my time and place and circumstance. I had bombarded my image with these historical facts, and they had stuck.

What I still did not know exactly was why she was running, but it seemed likely that she had been attacked, hurt in some way. *But there was, more so than ever, something about this girl that had not been changed by a bitter experience.* She had a great capacity for love, a quality of stubbornness that came through in the way she kept going, in spite of physical exhaustion. She would not be affected by hysteria. She represented something admirable in the human spirit.

It would have been at about this stage that I consciously compared my image of Miss Manners, in her probably historical context of the riots of 1942, with the mission school superintendent who was dragged from her bicycle in the riots of 1919, and knew that a missionary was exactly what Miss Manners was not, although, in the book, she does indeed have a bicycle whose presence in a ditch is part of the plot. But I began to think of a missionary and to invest that missionary with qualities I felt were different from but perhaps complementary to those of the girl. This I call going in through the back of the

87

image. It is a technique of reverse exploration; it creates scenes and situations that are variations of those of the original image. It is a technique of comparison. It is a way of giving balance to different aspects of a narrative, a way of giving form and shapeliness to the whole and extra significance to each of the parts thus compared. It can also be a method dictated by despair. I somehow despaired of finding that girl in the image continuing. Don't despair of despair. It is a symptom of your creativity.

My mission school superintendent is a far more contrived figure than Daphne Manners, a much more conscious creation. Incidental characters usually are. Even so, she didn't come alive for me until I first saw her performing an unexplained act I might regard as typical. I saw her taking down from the wall of her bungalow a portrait of her old hero, Mr. Gandhi. That would have been about April 1942. Well, there she was, a half-baked elderly English liberal making a half-baked gesture. And the image of the picture being removed created another of a picture that stayed up—an old engraving showing Queen Victoria receiving tribute from representatives of her Indian empire. The title of the picture was "The Jewel in Her Crown." The whole history of my missionary was suddenly revealed by her possession of these pictures, her history, and her attitudes, her good intentions, her liberal instincts, her failure emotionally to cross the bridge between East and West. The book suddenly could begin *behind* the image of a girl who *had* crossed the bridge between East and West.

As for the girl, so for Miss Crane, my missionary, the climax comes at the outset of the riots in August 1942. Hearing that the riots have broken out, she returns the seventy-five miles from an outlying school she's responsible for, accompanied by an Indian teacher who insists on protecting her. They are stopped at a lonely spot by a gang of hooligans. The Indian is dragged from the car and murdered. Miss Crane is knocked into a ditch. When she recovers consiousness her little car is burnt out, the rioters have gone, Mr. Chaudhuri is lying dead in the road. It is beginning to rain. Hurt, frightened, but courageous, Miss Crane begins to walk to find help, thinking, "There's nothing I can do." Walk, you see, not run. And it is daylight, not dark. But suddenly she knows there *is* something she can do, even though it is too late. She walks back to Mr. Chaudhuri, sits on the roadside and holds his hand—one human being making contact with another. One is black, one is white. One is dead, the other alive. It is negative, useless, stupid, but—in its context, *right*—the novel is away. Going in through the back of the original image has begun to unlock its mysteries, and in this particular case—and each novel you write is a different case—*by leading up to the climax of the riots it has suggested that the form the novel will take is that of approach,* through different eyes, through different histories, from different vantage points of time—to a central point of reference, which is exemplified in the original image—the action of that image and the implicit emotional content of that image.

Yes, truly, Miss Manners is in love with her Indian—and he with her, and she would not limit the expression of it to holding his hand when he is dead. They could not, of course, have chosen a worse time, a worse place, to be in love with each other. It was my job to explore the reactions of many different people to that time and those circumstances. The image had exploded in all its complexity; it was my job, somehow, to recontain it. Once I had seen what it was, it was a comparatively easy book to write. They aren't always. Your original image may not respond at all to this technique of approaching it from the back, and it may not contain those elements, as this one did, of specific historical circumstances which will illuminate it. There are two-hundred thousand words or more in *The Jewel in the Crown.* There are two third-person narratives—the story of Miss Crane, the missionary, and the story of poor ill-fated Hari Kumar. There are three characters who speak their recollections to a narrator who is really myself—Lili Chatterjee, whom Daphne Manners was staying with; Sister Ludmila, a now-blind old woman who ran a refuge for the homeless and the dying at the time of the riots; and Robin White, who was the deputy commissioner for the district. There is one statement, in the form of a deposition taken from a young Indian arrested for subversive activities, and there is an extract from the soldierly memoirs of Brigadier Reid, whose job it was to control the riots when the civil authorities could no longer control them. There is a description by the narrator of an evening spent in the club twenty years after the events which once filled it with the chatter of the British colony. Finally there is the journal kept by poor Miss Manners after Hari has been wrongfully arrested for the criminal assault on her and imprisoned under the Defence of India rule as a political undesirable—a journal in which she records the truth of the events of that particular night that ended with her running along all those deserted, ill-lit roads.

If you analyze the book, piece by piece, you would find many examples of the uses to which my experience and knowledge have been put. For example:

The mothers thanked Miss Crane for returning the children safely and offered her some tea, which she drank by the roadside, sitting on a chair they brought out and put under a tree. Two or three children gathered round her—a mother came with a plate covered by a napkin. Beneath it there were piping hot chappatis. The sweat was forming on her forehead. It was so hot and humid. While she ate the people stood watching. I hate it, she thought, I've always hated it, this being watched, like something in a zoo, seated on a chair, under a tree, by the roadside.

That describes my own feelings waiting for the bus, but it is used here to *show* us something about Miss Crane. An hour later she is holding the dead Indian's hand. The first image illustrates her good intentions, her inability to lose self-consciousness as a white person in a black person's world. The second image illustrates that too, but also shows her gesture of attempted amendment. Both images are related to the main one of the girl running in darkness, because the girl who runs is one who has stepped out of the closed safe little circle of her kind.

This is an example of the use of *experience* in relation to the central situation. An example of the use of knowledge *plus* experience can be found in the recollections of the deputy commissioner whom I have used—in effect as something of a mouthpiece for my own political and historical ideas, in other words my *knowledge* in the sense I've previously defined it. At one point, White recalls the moment when, as a very junior official, he fell in love with India and with his job:

My bowels were in a terrible state and I couldn't face anything, let alone toddy. I was lying on a charpoy, without a mosquito net, and suddenly saw this middle-aged Indian woman standing in the doorway watching me. When our eyes met she made namaste and then disappeared for a moment, and came back with a bowl of curds and a spoon.

I was on my dignity at once, and waved her away, but she came to the bedside and spooned up a helping of the curds and held it out and made me eat, just as if I were her nephew or son and needed building up. She said nothing and I couldn't even look at her—only at her black hands and the white curds. Afterwards I fell asleep and when I woke up I felt better and wondered whether I hadn't dreamed it all, until I saw the bowl of unfinished curds covered with a cloth, on a brass tray by the bedside and a flower on the tray next to the bowl. It was morning then, and the settlement officer was snoring in the other bed. I felt that I had been given back my humanity, by a nondescript middle-aged Indian woman. I felt that the curds and the flower were for affection, not tribute, affection big enough to include a dash of well-meant motherly criticism, the suggestion that my indisposition could be overcome easily enough once I'd learned I had no real enemies. I remember standing in the open doorway and breathing in deeply; and getting it; the scent behind the smell. They had brass pots of hot water ready for my bath. . . . Later I looked among the women but couldn't tell which of them had come into the hut the night before and fed me as she would have fed her own son. There was another flower on the pommel of my saddle. It embarrassed me. But I loved it too. I looked at the settlement officer. He had no flower and hadn't notice mine. As we rode away I looked back, and waved. The people made no move in reply, but I felt it coming from them—the good wish, the challenge to do well by them and by myself. I've never forgotten that.*

Now contrast that with a similar recollection by the Brigadier Reid, whose attitude to India is quite different:

When I looked out on to the *maidan* from the window of my room in the old artillery mess in Mayapore, or drove round the cantonment, I could not help but feel proud of the years of British rule. Even in these turbulent times the charm of the cantonment helped onto bear in mind the calm, wise and enduring things. One had only to cross the river into the native town to see that in our cantonments and civil lines we had set an example for others to follow and laid down a design for

---

*Editor's note: No quotation from Robin White appeared in Scott's text, but Scott's use of a page number in conjunction with the context of the novel and knowledge of the character make it clear this was the moment Scott had quoted. Whether he quoted more or less from the section is not clear.

civilised life that the Indians would one day inherit. It seemed odd to think that in the battle that lay ahead to stop all this from falling into the hands of the Japanese, the Indians were not on our side.

White has a sense of obligation to the Indians he rules; Reid's sense is more that of the obligation the Indians are under for the benefits of white rule. Each attitude is reflected in that of the missionary, Miss Crane. Both are comments upon the central situation of the girl, who, falling in love with an Indian, attempted to associate with him simply as a human being. When it comes to it—and I don't intend to give the whole thing away—we find that she is running to *save* that association, *not running away from it*. She writes in her journal, months later:

> I said: "There's nothing I can do, nothing, nothing," and wondered where I'd heard those words before, and began to run again, through those awful ill-lit deserted roads that should have been leading me home but were leading me nowhere I recognised; into safety that wasn't safety because beyond it there were the plains and the openness that made it seem that if I ran long enough I would run clear off the rim of the world.

This illustrates something else important about the image of the girl running. There is not just the question of why she is running but of the place she is running. Here I am using the immensity of India to say something about the littleness of the individual human attempt to make an impression on the world as we know it, and this in turn is meant to say something about the frailty of individual human action in the face of pressures exerted by a collective conscience—what I call the moral drift of history. When Daphne says she feels that if she ran long

93

enough she would run clear off the rim of the world, she is echoing that first paragraph:

> Imagine then, a flat landscape, dark for the moment, but even so conveying to a girl running in the still deeper shadow cast by the wall of the Bibighar Gardens an idea of immensity, of distance, such as years before Miss Crane had been conscious of, standing where a lane ended and cultivation began.

The idea of immensity, of distance, was not perhaps explicit in the original image, but it was implicit. I had to subject the image to the slow process of creative exploration. And it is impossible, really, to analyze *that*, to say how *that* is done. You might say we do it to find out how. We never really do find out, and perhaps that explains why we go on trying. Tomorrow I shall be trying again, and some of you no doubt will be trying too. I wish us all good luck.

THE ARCHITECTURE
OF THE ARTS:
THE NOVEL

◆

["The Architecture of the Arts: The Novel" was Scott's morning lecture at a one-day school sponsored by Heinemann and held at Kingswood on October 10, 1967. Martin Esslin, drama critic and scholar, lectured in the afternoon. Scott considered his own text important enough on this occasion to revise and retitle it "Form and Function of the Novel," then deliver it during his lecture tour of India, 1972; and revise it again and deliver this later revision, under the same title, to the opening session of the twenty-fifth annual Writers' Summer School, Swanwick, 1973.

In this lecture, Scott explores some of the problems with literary abstractions like "form" and "the novel" as they are conventionally discussed. He shifts the conditions of the discussion to the properties of the materials out of which novels are made. Here, he uses Walter Allen's definition of a novel as a metaphor for the artist's vision of life and Bernard Bergonzi's description of a novel as a physical object to arrive at a discussion of novels as "edifices for human use."]

The theme of this one-day school is, if I may say so, very un-English. In this country it is bad form to talk about form—at least, in other than a horse-racing sense. I remember some years ago *The Observer* flew one of its Sunday-cultural kites by inviting prominent *English* writers and critics to express their views about the future of the novel, with special reference to its form and shape. They were given plenty of space—at least one hundred words each. That it was enough was proved by Mr. Kingsley Amis's admirably brief response, "Form and shape? I thought we'd finished with all that."

That we have "finished with all that" is not, of course, quite true. But that is still a pretty esoteric subject—as my talk will no doubt prove, when we find ourselves moving further and further away from that comfortable-sounding word *architecture*, with its suggestion of a vision translated into a precise geometry from which the vision is reconstructed as an edifice for human use, which is more or less how architecture is defined by dictionaries.

Fundamental to the novel is a vision, certainly, but its geometry is far from precise, it is not mostly an edifice, and sometimes I wonder whether it is any longer for *human* use. These, as you will recognize, are the preliminary defensive remarks of a person actually engaged in writing novels, flushed on a Sunday morning out of his study, where he spends a great deal of time writing about things that have never happened, to entertain people most of whom he will never meet. There are times when it strikes one as a highly unintelligent occupation of which the less said, the better; times when it seems unlikely that anything as definite as the architecture of its end product can be discussed at all.

At this stage, then, I'm going to throw out the word *architecture* as one that produces a too-rigid image of something visible and demonstrable. For much the same reason, let's throw out the word *shape*, as well. We may—who knows—come back to both, but through the back way, not the front door. That leaves us with *form*, a happily and paradoxically amorphous word. But, on this English Sunday morning, before we begin to feel too exposed to that quaint little draft most of us are conscious of blowing on the back of our necks whenever someone mentions anything that might remotely turn out to be a branch of aesthetics, we'll posit—if only from the premise that a bottle is

96

shaped the way it is to hold the liquid poured out in discrete measures—that *form is inseparable from function*, which latter is defined by the Oxford English Dictionary as the mode of action by which something fulfils its purpose. That is a good, four-square, nonintellectual idea. Function. And of course the notion of its function is as much a part of the form of the novel as it is part of that of a building.

Unfortunately, with novels there is not the same degree of certainty about function or purpose as there seems to be in other fields of art. On the whole, I am delighted that there is not. It makes for variety. How dull life would be if all novelists were agreed on the question of what a novel is—not dull only because they might then all write the same kind of books, but also because they would have no opportunity to entertain us with their public and private clashes of temperament.

Tolstoy and Turgenev never quite saw eye to eye about the purpose of fiction. Turgenev admired Tolstoy's work but had reservations, and in any case the admiration was not mutual. Tolstoy thought that the older man was too *much* devoted to the art of the novel and too *little* devoted to life and the purpose to which the novel could be put in the sphere of social and moral education. There was once a fierce quarrel, and the ominous likelihood of a dual. For years they didn't speak. But in 1878, when he was sixty and Tolstoy was fifty, Turgenev visited the count's household.

They discussed religion and philosophy. Turgenev played chess with one of the children and, as a treat, read the family a tale he had written. This was received politely but without burning enthusiasm. The two novelists then went for a walk. They came across a seesaw. Looking at the seesaw and then at each other, they were aware of a subtle challenge that each found irresistible. Turgenev mounted one end and Tolstoy the other, and then they were at it, up and down, up and down, faster and faster—one moment Turgenev and *his* ideas in the ascendant, the next Tolstoy. Of course the Tolstoy children were delighted. As we may be, too, not only with the image of the two distinguished gents playing games, but also with the visual acting-out of the ups and downs of literary principles and reputations.

Bernard Shaw once said to Joseph Conrad, "Your novels just won't do, you know," which nearly led to another duel. Dickens and Thackeray hated each other. Wells lampooned Henry James. Attending the funeral of Sir Hugh Walpole, his archenemy Somerset Maugham is said to have remarked, "This is the first public function dear Hugh and I have attended together for years."

In 1938, Cyril Connolly wrote: "Strachey, Galsworthy, Bennett, Lawrence, Moore, and Firbank are dead and also out of fashion. They are as if they had never been. Suppose new manuscripts were discovered, a Five Towns by Bennett, a Forsyte by Galsworthy, even another novel by D. H. Lawrence. It would be a nightmare." That is a quotation from a book he wrote as an inquiry into the problem of how to write a book which lasts ten years. It was called *The Enemies of Promise*, which he listed as politics, conversation, drink, casual sex, journalism, and worldly success. As a writer I am threatened by several of these but not by others—which I shall significantly fail, in both cases, to enumerate. But perhaps I may add one enemy to Mr. Connolly's list—the failure to perceive that you may define the function of novels, but never the function of The Novel. The Novel. Is there any such thing? The building, the poem, the play, the painting. In those cases the definite article merely looks ridiculous. Applied to novels it attempts to establish collective grandeur out of the enforced association of disparate objects. When people talk about The Novel, the vision that I have is of a sort of literary St. Pancras Station, which some well-meaning fellows have formed a society to preserve as a monument of historical interest and importance. But this is not the vision *they* have. When they talk about The Novel, they see, I suppose, something in the nature of a giant, pulsating animal structure in a constant state of reformulation, gifted with chameleon properties, and contorted with the pains of indigestion following the eating of its own dead matter and with the pangs of parturition as it ejects with elephantine labor the egg of the new matter that will, in turn, eat *it*. Constantly changing but at any moment definable with a zoological exactitude as to habits, diet, and purpose and as to the degree it successfully performs the duties its present appearance suggests are those most fitted to it.

Well, so far I'm not doing very well, I'm afraid. I've thrown out architecture, suspended shape, and am now even denying the existence of what I've come to talk about, The Novel. A somewhat negative score, and my confidence in making a positive one is undermined somewhat when I look at what I'm left with—function, and a history of violent disagreement about what it is.

Fortunately—Tolstoy and Turgenev apart—there has been *some* measure of agreement, even if it is not always conscious. Let's look at what various writers have said about novels in the past one hundred years or so:

"We find here," wrote Hazlitt, "a close imitation of man and manners, we see the very web and texture of society as it really exists, and as we meet it when we come into the world. . . . We are brought acquainted with the motives and characters of mankind, imbibe our notions of virtue and vice from practical examples, and are taught a knowledge of the world through the airy medium of romance."

"Prose fiction," wrote Henry James in two Jamesian sentences, the second of which will require a deep breath, "now occupies itself as never before with 'the condition of the people,' a fact quite irrelevant to the nature it has taken on. Works of art are capable of saying more things to man about himself than any other works whatever are capable of doing—and it's only by saying as much to him as possible, by saying, as nearly as we can, all there is, and in as many ways and on as many sides, and with a vividness of presentation that 'art' and 'art' alone is adequate mistress of, that we enable him to pick and choose and compare and know, enable him to arrive at any sort of synthesis that isn't through all its superficialities and vacancies, a base and illusive humbug."

"For our time," wrote Lionel Trilling, "the most effective agent of the moral imagination has been the novel of the last two hundred years—its greatness and its practical usefulness is in its unremitting work of involving the reader himself in the moral life, inviting him to put his own motives under examination, suggesting that reality is not as his conventional education has led him to see it. It was the literary form to which the emotions of understanding and forgiveness were indigenous, as if by the definition of the form itself."

More recently, Mr. Ronald Bryden wrote in the *Spectator*: "It's no good pretending we can still believe in novels—not as the Victorians took Trollope and George Eliot, seriously as life. We can no longer suspend disbelief for one man's voice announcing, 'Here is the World.' Worlds, perhaps. We admit Proust's, Faulkner's, Anthony Powell's—but those are something smaller and less enfolding. To maintain its weakened hold on some kind of reality, fiction has shrunk to private visions, single lives, moods, incidents; from the empire conquered by Dickens, Balzac, and Tolstoy to the provinces of the short story. When plays stopped pretending to be life, they could begin to be serious statements about reality. Something similar is happening at last in the novel. Novelists are beginning to treat the novel frankly as what it has always been: a toy, a miniature, a puppet-show model."

Through those quotations it would be easy to trace the function of novels as changing, developing, declining—whichever you choose—from the lively moral sermon to the private joke. Well, there seems to be some truth in that. What, on the face of it, could be a bigger private joke than the work of a young avant-garde writer that comes in boxed but unbound pages, that the reader reads in any order he likes?

Or, take another example, Julio Cortázar's *Hopscotch*, which the author recommends you to read in one of two ways—from page 1 to page 349, ignoring pages 350 to 564, or starting at chapter 73 and following the instructions at the end of each chapter to turn to another chapter which is anywhere but on the following page.

This long novel of Cortázar's costs thirty-five shillings, but there is no fifty-percent refund offered if you select the half-measure. That isn't funny—unlike the joke Mr. Nabokov played in *Pale Fire*, which, he said, not without justification, you need two copies of if you're going to have a comparatively easy time with it.

Is the fold-in, the loose-page, the cut-out, the double-banked book, a novel? How can we say it isn't except by arbitrarily choosing—as definitive of novels—those which comply with more familiar rules for printed prose narrative? For example, Dame Rebecca West's *The Birds Fall Down*. Is that a novel? How can we say no except by arbitrarily reversing the process of comparison in say, Cortázar's favor, and saying Dame Rebecca's is a dead form and his is new and alive? In either case, if we choose, aren't we detaching form from function, admiring or detesting shape as shape, without asking ourselves, Why is it *that* shape? without asking ourselves, What is this book's function? And if we do ask ourselves what is this book's function, should we find that there is something in the function common to both books? Something which, once admitted, will help us to a definition of what novels are and so to an understanding of the problems of their construction?

Well there *is* something in novels that can be seen as a common factor, or common function. Let's look at a synthesis of the views of Hazlitt, James, Lionel Trilling, and Ronald Bryden.

> We see, in novels, the very web and texture of society as it really exists and as we meet it when we come into the world. Works of art, such as novels, are capable of saying more things to a man about himself than any other works are capable of doing. The greatness of the novel is in its unremitting work of suggesting to the reader that reality is not as his conventional education has led him to see it. To maintain its hold on reality, fiction has now shrunk to private visions, single lives, moods, incidents.

Well, of course, I've cheated a bit; Hazlitt's airy romance has gone, along with James's contention that the condition of the people is irrelevant to the nature of novels. Trilling's reference to the moral life and fiction's practical usefulness has been ignored. Bryden's weakened hold has lost that value judgment implicit in the word *weakened,* and he has been deprived of his contention that we no longer suspend disbelief for one man's voice announcing, "Here is the world." No author has ever said *that,* in my opinion, but only, "Here is my world." That the world's modern novelists see have externally diminished in comparison with those seen by the Victorians is perhaps a less controversial statement.

But I don't apologize for cheating, because by doing so I wonder whether something very simple but very important has been clarified—the common factor: the reference by Hazlitt to society as it really exists, by James to the more things about himself that the novel tells a man, by Trilling to a novelist's capacity for showing a reader a reality that is not conventional reality, by Bryden to the novel's hold—weakened or otherwise—on some kind of reality. The common factor is not the moral sermon, art for art's sake, or a private joke. The factor admitted by these critics as common to the idea of novels is the word *reality*, the idea of it, and by deduction, the question—*of what does reality consist?*

The theory that the function of novelists is to expose to the public view their private visions of what constitutes reality is not new, although it is often overlooked as a primary consideration in discussing the function of *novels*. Mr. Walter Allen, I think, expressed it awfully well when he said that every novel is an extended metaphor of the author's view of life—a working model of life as he sees it and feels it. Mr. Allen also foreshadowed Mr. Bryden's references to novels as toys, puppet shows, in the following passage, which I quote from his book, *The English Novel*: "Part of the impulse that drives the novelist to make his imitation world must always be sheer delight in his own skill in making: Part of the time he is, as it were, taking the observed universe to pieces and assembling it again for the simple and naive pleasure of doing so. He can no more help playing then a child can."

There are two points to make about this theory of a novelist's function. The first is that it sounds almost too obvious, too vague, too undefined. The second point is that the vagueness and obviousness make it difficult to distinguish a novelist's function from that of any other artist. *To expose to public view his private vision of what reality is:* You could say that *is* the function of any artist.

Taking the first point—the apparent lack of real definition—the trouble is, if you seek a clearer definition, you begin to narrow the area that the novelist is permitted to exploit. For instance, if you introduce the question of the moral purpose to which novels can be put, you are in danger of imposing on their function an internal discipline, and if you impose a discipline on the function you begin to impose one on the form, since the two are inseparable. If your novel is to have a moral purpose, then rather too readily it begins to follow that its form should be made easily accessible to anyone who will benefit from its lessons. A novel may have a moral effect, but it is dangerous to regard that, or any other external effect, as part of its essential function. The novelist may so regard it—Tolstoy did and wrote very considerable novels—but the readers of novels, I think, should not look for anything in function that narrows this vague definition: a view into a private vision of reality.

Which brings us to the second point: that this definition of a novel's function will do pretty well for any form of creative endeavor in what are called "the arts." And so it will. But at this stage we come up against the primary aspect of *form as it relates to function,* and this primary aspect *is* a discipline imposed from outside. It is the one part of form which is ready-made, which ostensibly controls the artist's form by imprisoning it in certain artificial but real-enough channels. The painter's vision of reality is imprisoned by a canvas of specific dimensions, the sculptor's by the physical properties of the material he works in. The imprisonment of the literary arts varies. Plays have one kind of formal prison, novels have another.

The prison in which novels are confined is, of course, the book, which Bernard Bergonzi, in a recent Third Programme talk on this very subject of the possible effect of its physical externals on prose fiction, rather splendidly described as "a small, hard, rectangular object, whose pages are bound along one edge into fixed covers, and numbered consecutively." And he commented: "No matter how revolutionary a novel's content may become, it is still conveyed by a vehicle that has not essentially changed since the days of Defoe and Richardson."

As a practicing novelist, I have frequently been extremely conscious of the fact that the vehicle for my medium is, indeed, this small, hard, rectangular object, and it is good to hear it so described. The description may be dismissed by some as totally irrelevant and wholly philistine, but not by me. If form and shape, in the true inner sense, are elusive, the hard rectangular object is not. It is an excellent basis on which to begin to discuss the *problems* of a novel's construction.

The construction of *anything* is *controlled by the characteristics and properties of the materials available,* and the major characteristic of these materials is, I should say, that they are inert. Human creative activity is very largely a fight against this inertia— against the inertia of stone, paint, or—as in the novelist's case— the inertia of the printed word on paper, through which he attempts to convey the likeness of a vision that is mobile, audible, alive. At first flush, it may seem that he has advantages over a painter wrestling with a tube of paint, because words, after all, are expressions of thought, and one word alone may conjure for all who read it or hear it an infinite variety of complex active images, whereas a brushful of scarlet madder, stroked on the canvas, will merely leave a stain, a piece of itself. It is a direct transfer of inert material. It remains inert.

But, when you think about that, the worker in words has no such advantage. You might even say he is at a disadvantage. The finished painting or piece of sculpture, the complete building, enjoys, finally, the benefits of being made from inert material. It is there, the inert sum of its inert parts: real, visible, tactile, *usable.* It does not matter whether people do or don't enjoy looking at it or using it. It is a totality, and destructible only by time, accident, or deliberate attack. The artist in stone or paint may work comforted by this knowledge, the knowledge that he can stand back and see the whole of it staring back at him, an undoubted—if often a dubious—creation.

But the only thing *real,* visible, tactile, and usable about a novel is Mr. Bergonzi's small, hard, rectangular object, filled with pages that are filled with printed ciphers. And you could say that apart from its casual, decorative function on a coffee

105

table or bookcase, it does not begin to exist until someone picks it up and reads it, and that *then* it will exist not as the writer wrote it but as the reader reads it. It will exist as an illusory experience of the reader, which is a combination of what he receives and contributes, in an uncertain, temperamental state alternating between, or simultaneously consisting of, the active and passive frames of mind.

This is similar to the situation that exists between any work of art and its observer, but to an extent which the novelist *cannot*, the plastic or graphic artist can ignore the question of the *received* reality of his work, because the inert nature of the material he works with—which remains inert—settles the question for him. He does not need an active or passive reaction from someone else to demonstrate the existence of the work he has created.

Can the same be said of a novel? It is a debatable point, and it is debated. But the point is settled, I think, by deciding what form a novel has that is never read by anyone except the writer. It will have two forms: first, the imprisoning form of its material shape—a bound and printed book, or pile of holograph pages; and, secondly, the form as it exists in the writer's mind—a series of mobile, audible images, so arranged as to express a formal image of his view of reality. Are these two forms enough?

I think not. You might put it as simply as this: that except as an *aide-mémoire* for its originator, the transference of those images to the page serves no useful purpose *in itself*. The author has, continually, his ideas, notions, images of the reality of life. By putting them on paper he is *not* performing the same function as an artist is, putting a plastic tactile substance on a sheet of canvas. The artist gets an immediate reaction from his manual activity. The writer does not, except to the extent that he looks at it as a reader. There is, therefore, a third and over-whelmingly important form in the novel, and that, of course, is the one whose function is communication to another person. I won't say that the other person is a piece of canvas the writer has designs on, because it sounds both mucky and immoral, and anyway isn't true. The writer and the reader between them make the marks, and they make them on a canvas that doesn't exist, they make them on a formless, almost indefinable area of consciousness that you could call the area of contact for the meeting of minds, the clash, the confrontation of wills and visions, and of physical and intellectual impressions of reality—the writer's and the reader's. *That this area of conduct should not be the scene of bored neutrality, still less of bored withdrawal,* is the main constructional problem a novelist faces. An imposing mansion is useless if the floors collapse and the roof caves in: That would be form without function. In a novel the function of the form is the dual creation by writer and reader of this area of involved, temperamental confrontation from which an image of reality emerges.

What reality?

We ought now to be rather more explicit about this vague but emotive word. When discussing a literary artist's vision of reality, we mean his idea of the reality of his human experience, *human* reality. Human reality is not by any means always the same as literary reality, but literary reality is, I think, inseparable from human reality. The components of the literary artist's vision differ from those of the workers in plastic and graphic arts. These latter are interested in the nature of *things*, of natural phenomena: forms, light, density, textures—including those of the human form and face. Their visions are *of the reality of matter.* It sounds an elementary point to make, but if we're not to be confused by the small, hard, rectangular object, or by evidence of apparently nonhuman reality entering literature in the shape of novels which deal with chairs, venetian blinds, the fall of a slant of light into the angle of a wall, it is well to make it.

The point about novels that seem to relate exclusively to *things* is that the things are depicted through the only medium possible to the form—language, the medium of direct human

107

communication of thought. Even if there sometimes appears to be no gloss of human emotion on the descriptions of these chairs and tables, you can't divorce the descriptions from the fact that they are human descriptions. We are invited to look at them through the eyes of another human being, and so, after all, a human emotion or idea is being conveyed, the idea perhaps, that man is trying somehow to reorientate to his surroundings. I cannot therefore say, and would not wish to, that works of prose fiction of this kind are not novels. They are. However obliquely they deal with a view of human reality, the use of words as a medium of expression at once rules out any other kind of reality.

Where have we got to? We're discussing—with certain, I hope, not uninteresting minor diversions—the characteristics and properties of the materials that are available to the novelist in the construction of his novel, and we began this discussion by positing that the construction, as in any other form of constructional activity, is largely controlled by the properties of those materials. But if we accept that a novel is a view on to the writer's vision of human reality, there is one material he uses whose properties are extremely difficult to enumerate. We begin now to leave the ground—to fly off from these interesting theories of the controlling influence of the hard rectangular object, its consecutive pages, and of the linear construction of printed language, of language itself—fly off, if only temporarily, from all such arguments as the retreat from the word, into the reality of what novels are in themselves, not the reality of how they are presented.

Since not everyone here is a writer—*at least I do hope not*—but almost certainly most are readers, let's look at novels, for the moment, from the reader's point of view. This is something which critics of novels seldom do, or if they do, consider it far too elementary a consideration to be worth noting as basic to the argument about what novels are.

The reader holds the rectangular objects. He turns the pages consecutively, unless he is reading a book by someone like Señor Cortázar. He is, certainly, being confronted by lines of printed words, which impose a linear order to the images he is conjuring up from his knowledge of the language. He may even be aware that a story has begun and is headed for a middle and possibly a logical end. He may be comforted or bored by that prospect. But when he comes to the end, what will he have in his mind? Every word in the book, in the sequence in which it was written? What a remarkable chap. And what a bore to talk to. The original literal man. I doubt he exists. What does exist is the man or woman to whom it has not mattered that the book was a hard rectangular object, filled with words set out in a certain order, *words which almost without exception he will have forgotten every one of.* What he does not forget, so readily, are the *impressions*, in the form of mobile, audible images—and it is very likely that presently no more than one or two of those images will remain. To him, what remains *is* the book. It is his experience of it.

Let's take a simple example, one that perhaps everyone in this room of my age upward will recognize as viable—one of the more romantic works of Charles Dickens, *A Tale of Two Cities.* To you readers, this novel may consist, recollectively, mainly in the last image of Sydney Carton mounting the steps to the guillotine. Oddly enough, Dickens never recorded directly the famous last words, "It is a far, far better thing," etc. But I would agree with you, because in that image there is the whole of Carton's history, the whole of Dickens's implied comment on the tragedy of a man like that—a very modern comment about a very modern man, if you think about it. Carton existed as a literary creation long before alienation and the search for identity came tripping off our tongues as explications of the human feeling of knowing you've got good in you somewhere if only you could find a way of bringing it out that other people would notice.

Carton at the guillotine, Lord Jim standing apart from his

fellow officers in the streets of Singapore, Constance Chatterley making her bosky way to the gamekeeper's cottage, the cry going up for "Esmiss Esmoor" from the crowd outside the courtroom in A *Passage to India*—these are what these novels are to a reader. They may be different things to different readers, but they will always be particularized and often solitary images of a human reality, exemplifying the book, yielding up what the book means to the reader.

The major problem the novelist has is so to construct his books as to provoke, in what I called that area of meeting or confrontation of his own and the reader's mind, a series of images from which the reader will extract a notion of human reality—corrupted as it must be by the reader's own notion, but nevertheless leaving a definite impression of identifiable human existence.

Two things follow: first, that the primary materials, from both the author's and the reader's point of view, are the images. Secondly, that because they are images—illusions of a mobile, audible, human activity—there are perhaps no actual *rules* to follow which will ensure they hold together, or to depart from which will lead to collapse. *You could say that because the images are not tactile, the question of their holding together simply doesn't arise,* except in so far as the author desires—and the reader demands—that the several images that make up the novel should be seen to bear some interesting and meaningful relationship to each other.

But the notion of what an interesting, meaningful relationship *is* will depend on what interests the author about this thing we call human reality, the thing about it which—rather playfully—he wishes to expose by taking it to pieces in his mind and reassembling it in a way that *will* expose it.

When we talk about the growth or development, the past, the present, and the future of the novel—which I'm afraid we often do—what we're really talking about is not the growth and development of its *function* (which is a constant—to expose a private view of human reality), but the growth and development of interest in different aspects of that reality, and of a novelist's ability to deal adequately with them.

As our interests grow more complex, more sophisticated, or simpler, so do our images. So too—although it does not necessarily follow—will the notion of what is their interesting relationship to one another. It depends on the particular view of human reality, how complex that relationship can become. A man who is concerned with the realities of power as it may affect men who hold positions in public life is likely to find himself involved in a less complex relationship of images than is the man who is concerned with the realities of, say, time as part of the human experience. The one is likely to be content with the disciplines of linear construction, the other at pains to bend that construction in order to convey through a less formal relationship of images something of what he is trying to convey about that time.

We are now beginning to talk about shape. We are getting perilously close the the mechanics—perilously, because at this stage, considerations such as how images are to be transferred to the page, with what words, in what order, for what reasons, begin to emerge and bring in their wake considerations such as the restrictions of language with its tradition of logic and forward movement, and its gross omissions in conveying the fullness of what is seen and thought and felt, and comprehended.

There are, as you know, current philosophies that not only posit the end of the printed word as a viable means of communication but see it as having been, by and large, an obstruction to our social development. There are disapproving arguments that link the growth of novels to the growth of the printed word, much as the growth of violence is linked, sometimes, to the invention and development of television. Well, I'm sure we are all committed to drift toward some audiotactile utopia, and I regret I shall not live to see it, much as I regret I did not live long enough *ago* to see a dodo. But for the moment, as a novelist, I am concerned with the exercise of my craft, as it seems to me exercisable *now*, and over the next few years.

But when the freedoms of a medium are questioned and its limitations exposed—when you are conscious of them as they affect you in your day-to-day work—you're bound to think about them. And it occurs to me that one effect of the invention of the printed word was to extend, far more broadly than the written word could do, the conditions under which human ideas could be communicated in silence, and between no more than two people at a time—the writer and the reader—and that this was not an entirely bad thing. The empathy that can exist between two people is of a different order than that existing in a crowd, and the condition of silence in which the reader reads and confronts the writer's images allows him a more active role. Written words take the rhetoric out of language, they cut the swank, the persuasive pressures of actual audibility. They can also, of course, cut out the boredom. Dangerously, I take the example presently in front of you. But, bored or not bored, there is no doubt that your response to what I'm saying is different from what your response would be if you were reading in print, in private, the words I'm speaking, and the words I've written *for* speaking would themselves then not be exactly the same words. For instance, it would not be necessary to make little jokes to help you to relax.

Of course the written language has its own rhetoric, its own brand of swank, and its own power to persuade the reader into a captive, passive role; and this capacity of the written language and printed word *is* a danger, like that of oratory, particularly if novelists and the readers of novels look to novels as things that can provide a *definitive* experience which it is the novel's duty to create and demonstrate in use.

The danger of the printed word does seem to lie in its appearance of self-sufficiency, its look of immaculate conception, of containing a given truth, of enciphering a demonstrable fact, of embodying an idea there is only one interpretation of. In sequence these printed words establish an illusion of conveying hard information. A novelist is very often conscious of their power to reduce his ideas to a formula, and the reader may easily be hypnotized by them into a state of vegetable acceptance, with the result that the desired end—of the creation of an area of contact between writer and reader, in which the former's images of human reality are activated by the reader's own creative response to them—does not take place.

Some novelists, of course, intend that it should not. They are there to *tell*, like pedagogues. And many readers entirely fail to comprehend that they are being asked to give as well as receive. Whether the invention of printing is wholly to blame for this state of affairs I don't know. The world, it seems to me, has always been full of both pedagogues and freeloaders, so I'm inclined to think not.

But the state of affairs does have an important bearing on the problems of construction. Aware of the various disciplines which his images of reality will be subjected to before they reach the area of contact, the novelist may well fight tooth and nail to bend them, knowing as well that to bend the disciplines and be seen to bend them may jolt the reader out of his passivity, force him to take part. These disciplines are the book, the printed word, the linear construction of language, the consecutive nature of a narrative that conveys a logical sequence of thought, the discipline of logic itself. Bending these disciplines will produce novels that play tricks with typography, that have no apparent logical sequence, that you are invited to read backward, forward, or sideways as the spirit moves you. It will also produce novels with blank pages and holes cut in the middle.

But the one thing they all have in common is that they all have to be looked at and—unless presently we have a novel entirely composed of blank pages—they all have to be read, *read in whatever order*. I applaud the existence of novels like this for the job they do of jolting the reader out of his passive role, and for whatever additional provocation they set up in the area of contact. I do not applaud them for widening the function of novels, because they have not done that. They may have helped draw attention back to it, and each one in itself may demonstrate the power which shape—or shapelessness—has to guide the reader to the areas of contact in which the particular vision of human reality is to be seen. But the function of novels remains as performable *only through words read in silence*. Throw out that function as inadmissable in human society, and you throw out novels. It may come. It has not yet. For the moment we are stuck with them, and with the problem of how to make them for the use which is appropriate to them.

We are talking, you may remember, about the materials available, each of which has its controlling characteristic: Perhaps we can now enumerate them, in descending order of importance. There are three. First, there are the images which contain the author's notions of human reality, no doubt populated for the most part with characters performing actions, thinking thoughts, and setting up an interplay of reaction between each other and their environment, all of which play some part in revealing what the author thinks of as real about their situation and his own. Second, there is the language in which the images are encoded; third, the material means by which the encoding is made available for decoding.

This sounds pretty bleak, and in one way it is. The writer works downwards from an image to a small, hard rectangular object. The reader attempts to reverse the process. It's all very obvious, but that's what happens, so it's as well to be clear about it.

But there is another consideration, very pertinent to the subject of the design and construction of novels. What do you do to *persuade* the reader to reverse the process? In building terms, this is a cross between using an available material and keeping function in mind, a cross between cementing your bricks to keep your building up and remembering to provide a door to let people in to use it. I've already suggested—naively enough—

that the overwhelmingly important aspect of the form and function of a novel is communication with another person. What available material is there that will persuade a reader to be communicated with, that will help to hold your edifice up, reveal the relationship of your images, and allow him access to all of them?

I suppose there are many things that will persuade: his own curiosity, the brilliance of the images, the fascination of the situations—but these are questions of luck, talent, and choice. They are not materials in the real sense of the word. The cementing material, so it seems to me, must be something common to the language and to the relationship between the separate images—a material which both writer and reader are in possession of, and have a common understanding of, one using it to create and the other to recreate.

Before an idea can be conveyed in speech, it has to be assembled in some kind of order. The linear construction of language may reduce an image to a linear formula, but it is a formula that enables a reader in possession of the same formula to work back from it to the same order of assembly. The logic is not in the language but in the assembly of thoughts, and there seems to be something in man that urges him to assemble his thoughts tidily, to impose order out of the confusion of what he is *capable* of thinking, if only in order to know what he is thinking now. A novel composed entirely of words which are totally unrelated by a chain of thought—*Cat cloud sink club fieldglasses (and if we haven't had one yet I have a simply horrid feeling that we're going to)* would be a rather tedious exercise in the association of ideas, and the reader would associate them in an entirely different way than the writer. It would not be a novel because it would not give us a view onto *its author's* view of human reality. I mean one doesn't go round thinking "Cat cloud sink club fieldglasses." At least I don't think so. I am open to suggestion on this matter. But in the absence of proof to the contrary, I should say that our thoughts are more logically assembled directly we succumb to the urge to think them or even more—to the temptation to convey them.

Perhaps *this* is play, play with the abstractions which are our thoughts, but we all know the rules of the game. Certainly an element of play enters when we begin to use the cement of logic in relating our novel's images to each other. If the logic of the written and printed word is sometimes a straitjacket, forcing the writer into a statement the reader will take as hard information—take seriously in life—the tricks an author can get up to in juxtaposing the images are many and varied. He can break the old formulas, startle the reader, force him to adjust to multiple and apparently illogical changes of time and place without disrupting the purely mechanical process of pages consecutively turned. And of course novelists have *always* done this. Switching the center of interest chapter by chapter is not different, in intention, from switching it within a single sentence—a ruse I have never resorted to myself because I have never found a point so subtle that the discipline of the sentence's chain of reasoning becomes unacceptable. And again, breaking an old formula merely involves setting up a new one. Gradually readers accept what were once startling formulas of presentation as not startling at all. Herein lies the great temptation: to startle the reader for the sake of doing so, not for the sake of the reality you're asking him to see, share, and contribute to the building of. Defiance of the logic of related images should never be complete. The logic is contained in the central idea of the reality that is being exposed. A book by Henry James composed of twelve chapters from twelve of his novels would almost certainly fail to convey an integrated view of his view of human reality. We come back, indeed, to the proposition that a novel is really *one* image—and in practice I've consistently found that this is so—and that the problem is not so much one of relating different images to each other but of digging into the central image to try to extract all its possible components, and then— and only then—trying to relate them back in what will be a logical order. It would be possible to display them always in a chronological order if their nature were always chronological. But their logic is not always apparent in terms of time or even of place. It will depend, in fact, on the nature of the image they're extracted from, on what aspect of human reality it is that I'm concerned with.

We return to my earlier remark that an interesting relationship of images depends on the particular view of human reality the author is at pains to show. I mentioned as examples a novel about the realities of power and one about the realities of time as part of the human experience. Both can be fine novels, but usually, the more accessible the idea, the more accessible the form. You might think it should be the other way round, and that complex visions should ideally be conveyed in simple narratives with traditional beginnings, middles, and ends. But there are difficulties. An author who is at pains to show the moment-to-moment flow of a person's thoughts during one day—that is to say, the reality of a man's total consciousness as opposed to the reality of his planned activity—is unlikely to find his images yielding much in the nature of what we call a story. And yet, perhaps, it would be perfectly feasible to create a plot out of the interplay of several characters' separate streams of consciousness. In fact we do so, because the stream of consciousness—admitted into the novel by writers like Dorothy Richardson, James Joyce, and Virginia Woolf—has been absorbed into novels, not, I suggest, as a technique which changed the *form* of novels, but as a *material*—as a new aspect of those human realities which are available to us to see, understand, and try to convey. Perhaps this example makes clearer my narrowing down of the function of novels to that simple definition of them as conveying a view of human reality. It is an unchanging function, and this means that its form is unchanging, variable only as the view of reality varies. To say that the stream-of-consciousness writers changed the form of the novel is to say that they changed its function, and that is tantamount to saying that only *their* view of human reality is now admissable. No wonder critics who say Joyce and Woolf changed The Novel also tend to say they brought It to an end.

I think the truth is that novels only change to the extent that human ideas of reality change, become more complex or even more simple. And to the extent that the writers of novels are men and women of their thinking times, the great novels will always memorably reflect that thinking, those views of what was thought real and therefore important about men and women in their social and historical environment.

In this talk on the architecture of novels—although I initially threw the word out as one that conjured an idea of too precise a geometry of constructional arrangement—I have tried to retain throughout an architectural *idea* of novels. I've said nothing about such things as character development, narrative techniques, peaks and troughs in action, the whole intricate rhythm of the parts in their relationship to the whole—because these are only the playful tricks the writer gets up to, to persuade his reader of the density and reality of the fabric of image which he wants the reader to look at and experience for himself. So many of the tricks, having served their purpose, are totally expendable. They are—like the words which are forgotten—as if they had never been.

I have not talked about proportion, except insofar as a sense of proportion may be allied to the human sense of logic, nor have I talked about the important part that sense of proportion plays in sustaining a scene, in getting the desired effect out of it, or in failing to sustain it or extending it beyond the point when it has been made. And anyway, that is mostly a question of trial and error. I have not talked, either, about the decorative flourishes that are style, the writer's tone of voice, which may be modest, strident, or somewhere in between.

But I have talked, I hope, about novels as edifices for human use; about the construction of this area of creative contact between two people, in private, in silence—an area of contact for consenting adults in the underworld of letters, utterly deprived of the benefits of collective persuasion, mob hysteria, the audiotactile love-in, the whole electronic heaven of instant shared response to the instant implacable *message* of whatever solitary *medium* it is that will be left to instruct us in what reality really is. I can hardly wait. Meanwhile we must go on, trying to make do with this other area. And reading novels *is* a creative occupation, whatever they say.

ENOCH SAHIB: A SLIGHT CASE OF CULTURAL SHOCK

♦

["Enoch Sahib: A Slight Case of Cultural Shock" was given as a luncheon address to the members of the Commonwealth Countries' League in London, November 11, 1969. According to a descriptive statement by the League, its work was carried out by means of conferences and social gatherings to inform and promote better relations among members of the Commonwealth, particularly visitors or newcomers to England.

In this address, Scott attacks insularity of a kind represented by Enoch Powell. Powell (1912–), a colorful figure in English politics, served in Parliament from 1950–74, representing Wolverhampton, an industrial city. A Conservative Member of Parliament, he spoke for white English citizens who feared "the coloured," those African and Asian peoples of the Commonwealth who immigrated to Britain. His solution for English problems related to these peoples was to send "the coloured" home. Scott relates "cultural shock" to prejudice of the kind Powell represents, then reveals his own susceptibility to it by telling of his stay in a village in Andhra Pradesh during a 1964 visit to India. He tells of his own erratic behavior and characterizes it as "understandable" but "not right." Finally he argues the need for international aid because it is humane].

The subject originally suggested for today was "India," but as you see from the rather curious title, India is not entirely what

121

I'm going to talk about. My reason for not doing so is best summed up by a quotation from an essay by Mr. Aubrey Menon. Mr. Menon writes:

> No more than two decades ago, a British comedienne would come on to a London stage dressed as a lady lecturer in a loose black gown. She would take a sip of water, hitch up a shoulder strap, clear her throat, and utter the word, "India." The audience would burst into a roar of delighted laughter. They laughed because India was a notorious bore. The lecture—which of course never proceeded—could only be about things which everybody knew and nobody wanted to hear again. India was a subcontinent, whatever that meant, inhabited by a rather excessive number of brown people. These people incessantly worshipped three thousand gods, would not kill cows, and even more eccentrically, would not kill human beings. They were divided into rigid castes that forbad all social progress. Women were treated as chattels and wives had to walk seven paces behind their husbands. From this benighted mass of people only two figures emerged—Mahatma Gandhi, who was a saint with the peremptory habit of refusing to eat when he could not get his own way, and Mr. Nehru, who regularly ate three meals a day and was a thorough gentleman. These two, with approximately four-hundred million fellow countrymen, statistically made up one-fifth of the human race, but it could not be said that it mattered very much.

I quote this interesting passage not only because I was taught that a well-fed audience will take longer to sink into a torpor if made to smile in the first minute, but also because what Mr. Menon says is, alas, only too true. To the British at home, India has always been high on the list of subjects that fail to arouse their curiosity.

122

While I do not believe for a moment that the British empire was acquired in a fit of absence of mind, absence of mind about it fairly described the attitude of those who took *no* part in acquiring or administering the countries that belonged to it. The same absence of mind can be seen today in regard to the whole strange semimystical, and very loose continuing association into which those countries have voluntarily come together—the association which gives your league its name. I am sure that if Miss Hermione Gingold—for it can only have been she—walked on to a London stage this evening in her loose black gown, with its unreliable support, opened her mouth, and said "The Commonwealth," the reaction of the audience would be precisely the same, with perhaps this difference—that some of the laughter would be more ironic than delighted, and, if among the audience there were a charabanc-load of people from, say, Wolverhampton, perhaps one block of seats whose occupants did not laugh at all.

Two decades ago and more, India was funny because it was far away and did not impinge. The British at home were always quite happy with their empire and quite happy to let it go, bit by bit, so long as they weren't pestered by it or about it. The Commonwealth, similarly, is a comfortable and warming concept, a splendid example to the world of interracial cooperation, and parts of it even offer salubrious homes-from-home to anyone who is inclined to have a change of scene and climate and so emigrate.

However, if you attempt to put into practice the theories which theoretically bind it together, and *start* pestering, by threatening to *impose* the theories in a practical manner, then people get nervous and start asking questions, and finding some of the possible answers. For instance, among these answers are the following: that the Commonwealth is a myth, has no reality, no substance—none, that is, which is visible to "the great majority of people in this country."

The words are those of the Right Honorable Member for

Wolverhampton South-West, Mr. Enoch Powell, and they are strong, forceful words. Or so they seem, out of context. But within context, I find something neither strong nor forceful, but a kind of miasma, which is defined as an infectious or noxious emanation, and the source of that emanation seems to be the thoughts and feelings not of Mr. Powell, but of what he calls "the great majority of people."

When it comes to selecting specimens of this majority, he always describes them, with that modesty that typifies an Englishman, as "ordinary, decent" men and women. Since I invariably find myself neither thinking nor feeling the same, I must presumably be described as extraordinary and indecent, or, to escape from the odium of such a definition, place myself among the small minority of people. But there I fare just as badly, particularly as someone in part-control of the means of communication, which would appear to be a very special mark of disgrace. Quite apart from that, though, I apparently subscribe to the absurd convention of ignoring the wide divergence between facts and aspirations, the inconsistencies between form and reality, between professions and deeds—or I shrug all that off as mere academics. In any case, I fail to see that these divergences and inconsistencies are leading us into actions and situations which are contrary to our manifest national interest. Therefore, I do not, have not had, my growing doubts crystallized into certainty by three recent episodes which, numbered, are (a) the visible menace of Commonwealth immigration, (b) the more harm than good done by aid to developing Commonwealth countries, (c) Rhodesia.

In regard to Rhodesia, if I were among the ordinary decent majority, I should resent being told that this must be done and that must be done, merely to stop the Commonwealth breaking up. I should mutter under my breath, "Let it break up, so much the better."

In adopting what you may detect as an ungrateful attitude toward Mr. Powell, I imagine I may not be alone in this room.

124

But I hope that in uttering the word "Enoch" I am not boring those of you, if there are any, who have decided that he may represent a large body of opinion but that it could not be said to matter much.

If he does represent such a body it matters a lot to me, and if he doesn't it still matters because the more he *says* he does, the more likely it is that he *will*. His target is the floating vote— a phenomenon that has puzzled many a politician but does not puzzle me. The floating vote is known to me personally. The floating vote is my aunt, the dear and ancient one who would vote for Mr. Powell tomorrow, even though she lives in the quiet of a seaside town where a brown face on the promenade would be as rare a sight as a dodo among the seagulls. Mr. Powell, she says, has such a *strong* face, and cares about *us*. My aunt was a great playgoer in her day. She is the kind who laughed at Miss Gingold's abortive lecture on India. But she laughed without malice. I am no longer sure that she would do so.

Mr. Powell has learned his history well. That absence of mind, that inattention to what is going on in the world, that insularity—all of which have distinguished the British race from races less entirely surrounded by water, like Piglet in *Winnie the Pooh*—have often, in the past, when things have been going right for them, given rise to the belief that their *government* should keep all the foreigners up to snuff and, if necessary, interfere with their business. When things are going badly, British insularity quickly promotes a passionate belief in the efficacy of everybody looking after his own.

Mr. Powell knows that recently things have been going none too well. He has shrewdly judged that a stern call to close the gate, lock the door, seal the windows, and sit in one's decent parlor on one's ordinary backside, counting the money, is likely to have the strongest possible appeal. I say shrewdly judged, because if he does not *see* the defeatism of the policies he advocates, he should go back and sit in the chair of Greek at Durham University. But I think he sees it—the appeal his policy has for others—as a means to the end of sitting in a seat of greater eminence.

The main title of this talk is perhaps now a little clearer. But by Enoch Sahib, I do not necessarily mean Mr. Powell. I mean any one of the people, like my aunt, in whom he has detected a readiness to withdraw from the problems of the modern world, and any one of the people in whom this spirit of withdrawal might yet be aroused. I also mean—for somewhat different reasons—myself.

India always did, still does, and probably always will bring out the Enoch in me. Mr. Powell has said that it is all very well to sit back in one's comfortable liberal home, far from those areas in which there are what he refers to as "evils" and "growing dangers." He does not himself say what *he* thinks those evils and dangers are. He tends to leave that to elderly women who write letters to him about curious objects shoved through letterboxes of homes they are being driven out of. He has skillfully manipulated racial arguments so that they emerge as the semi-articulate protests of worried or terrified people he felt it his plain duty to stand up for as spokesman, untainted himself by anything remotely like prejudice, untainted in fact by anything that can't be put down to the plain common sense of a man who will Sort Out the Mess and Get Things Done.

But the arguments, manipulated or not, aren't to be got rid of by throwing on them the sand of counterprejudice. You do not bury an unexploded bomb. You study it to identify its mechanism, and then try to render it harmless. So far as I'm concerned the primary area for study is oneself, since this is the only area from which one can report with any degree of accuracy.

I first heard the expression "cultural shock" in Hyderabad in 1964. It's of American origin and means the shock experienced by a man used to one form of civilization who finds himself in another quite different. It also means the shock a man has when an alien manner of life begins to appear within his own environment.

Cultural shock is not a new disease, merely a new concept, or explanation of an old symptom. It goes a long way to explain the form that Anglo-Indian society took in the days of the raj, and a similar long way to explain why today groups of immigrants, particularly of the artisan or unwesternized classes, tend to herd together. They do that for several reasons, but not the least of these is the need to be reassured that *their* world is still roughly the same shape. A little bit of Bharatpur in Birmingham is no different from a touch of Camberley in Calcutta. What repelled the caste Hindu there about Anglo-Indian manners and customs is the same as what repels a white fish-and-chips—eating native of Britain about mosques and temples and the smell of Rajasthani cooking.

Fear of the strange and alien, of losing one's sense of identity, is what causes like to cling to like. We should observe that ritual with sympathy. Unfortunately, such sympathy seems rare. The rituals are strange, and what is strange awakens the bad emotion of prejudice. In the face of prejudice, the immigrants will cling even more strongly, like to like. New arrivals find a community ready-made, and it is one in which they find enough comfort to feel little need ever to move outside it.

We observe this phenomenon, and some of us say, as Mr. Powell reported one of his constituents saying, "In fifteen years the black man will have the whip hand over the white." The situation is not eased when a black man suggests that this is precisely his intention. Our unknown constituent from Wolverhampton may well have evidence of arrogant speech and behavior—it is not exclusive to the British—but even if he hasn't such evidence and were here today, he would probably ask me at this point why, if the immigrants are half as shocked by our culture as he is by theirs, do they come in the first place, or having come, not go home.

If we disregard the memory that they were originally encouraged to come here, especially when prepared to do the kinds of job native members of our welfare state were increasingly reluctant to do, there are still many answers to that question, but I think common to *all* immigrants, in any direction, is the urge to widen the personal horizon, in the belief that by doing so something is gained apart from opportunities, skills, knowledge, money. It takes a certain amount of courage to set out from home, and it is a courage for which the world has always been a better place. Mr. Powell's constituent admires young white families who sell up and light out for Australasia. But no doubt, to him, because he hasn't stopped to think, the West Indian or Indian arriving here comes for the higher wage, the free false teeth, the national assistance, all the amenities lacking in the country of his birth, which of course it is convenient to forget was until recently and for a long time under our civilizing influence.

And that is another thing to remember about cultural shock. It is felt more strongly by people transplanted from a highly sophisticated society to one less sophisticated. A Punjabi peasant may be shocked, terrified, by the London underground, but he feels a certain awe. There is no awe to be struck in a Londoner by the sight and smell of untouchable encampments swimming in their own sewage on the road from Santa Cruz airport into Bombay. That he travels by car or bus along a modern dual carriageway heightens the sense of unreality, the suspicion that he has arrived in a place whose very air is dangerous to breathe and whose modernity is an illusion, calculated to drive him mad before it destroys him.

I think it would be true to say that when I go to India these days I suffer some degree of shock intermittently from the moment I arrive to the moment I leave. Sometimes I am actually physically afraid, at others wild with irritation. Recollections of bad behavior during a shock taint the periods of happiness and relaxation. For a man who would go back at the drop of a hat, these may sound curious confessions.

I went to India first during the war, like thousands of others. I knew nothing about it and didn't particularly care to. And of course I didn't go to India, I went to Anglo-India. The degree of shock was mild because Anglo-India was a ready-made and long-established community. Its cushions were extremely comfortable. I'm not at all sure that what cultural shock I suffered wasn't the shock of *Anglo*-India. The people weren't really my sort of people. I wondered where on earth they'd been, what doing, these past fifty years. The Indians I met socially were not many, and *they* seemed mildly shocked too. Without actually *dis*liking Anglo-India, I didn't *like* it. Some of it, in compensation, struck me as hilariously funny. But after I'd become used to it and my bowels had settled, India itself—the country and its people—nudged its way into my affection, and stayed there.

When I first went back, in 1964, I certainly didn't go looking for Anglo-Indian remains, and I didn't want to do the tourist run from one air-conditioned hotel to another. Neither did I want involvement with the High Commission or that body of splendid volunteers for overseas, the British Council. I wanted to get to know Indians. I heard that there were families who took in paying guests. Through my own publisher, a publisher in India undertook to arrange that. When I went out, I knew only the name of my first hostess in Bombay, and only after arrival discovered that I was her guest in the full sense of the word.

I found the same thing in each of the places I went subsequently. This extraordinary—but typical—Indian hospitality to a complete stranger did not surprise me. What did surprise me was the suspicion I discovered it arouses.

The only hotel I stayed at in 1964 was in Hyderabad, where I talked to a disgruntled Canadian woman who worked in Delhi. "You'll regret accepting their hospitality," she told me. "I did it once, but found there was a price attached. And then I was told there always is. So I've never tried to make Indian friends again."

If the Canadian woman's attitude had struck me as exceptional I would not mention it. But in fact it clarified and illuminated what I had already come to look upon as the sad scene of modern Anglo-Indian relations out there. At first, in going back, I was cushioned from the shock of India by the euphoria of just being back there, a state that was encouraged by the kindness of my hostess in Bombay. "What are you interested in?" she had asked me. "People and places," I said. For a week I met people, her closest friends, and we all went to places together. My stay in Bombay was for ten days. On the seventh she asked if there were anything particular I wanted to see that I hadn't. I thought for a moment and said, "It would be interesting for me to see some English."

She looked at her watch. It was midday. "That will be rather difficult right now," she said. "They'll all be in the permit rooms." (For those who don't know what a permit room is, I must explain that is is the licensed equivalent of an American speakeasy in the days of Prohibition. All leading hotels have permit rooms, and depressing places they are.) However, my hostess said we would see some English next day because we were going to Juhu and it was a Sunday.

We went to Juhu, and yes, there they were—the new race of sahibs and memsahibs—rather noisily segregated at one end of the hotel lounge. After lunch we called on an English friend of my hostess, a man who had stayed on in India. He had two Englishwomen visiting him. They spoke to me, but did not address a word to the Indians I was with, skillfully managed to avoid real introduction, and, when spoken to by one of the men, were afflicted by deafness.

In the car going home I broke into the general chatter and said: "I hope they aren't *all* like that?" That was a mistake. I have since learned that Indians prefer to ignore rudeness of this kind, to pretend that it doesn't happen.

But I was very angry. There were now supposed to be far more English in India than in the days of the raj, most of them out there on business, or as visiting experts on contract. The official picture was one of a free-mixing society, but the impression I was forming and presently formed was that, apart from those whose duties were of an ambassadorial nature, the rest, as in the old days, pretty much kept to themselves. Revelation that the Breach Candy swimming club was still run on a strict white-skin-only regulation did nothing to alter that impression.

In Madras I asked a young Brahmin engineer how he got on with his English colleagues. His answer was polite. I asked him for one that wasn't. That released the floodgate. They are all right when they first come out, he said, but in six months they are spoiled, because the others have got at them.

I stared, because what he had said came straight out of E. M. Forster. He thought my stare one of disbelief. He said, "Lunch with me at the executive canteen tomorrow and judge for yourself." I did so. He was right. The English executives sat at the top end of the table, the Indians at the bottom. The food was European style and quite uneatable. There was chaff, an illusion of free intercourse; but I had studied the English face in India long enough to recognize when a smile was not a smile, and a calm expression a mask to hide the feeling that one must protect oneself at all costs from being taken advantage of. And it was here that I detected another thing. Because I was with an Indian, I was treated by the other English with a special kind of reserve. Their faces said, "You've gone over. You'll be sorry."

Anglo-India is still alive and well and living in India. I know there are exceptions, because I have met a few. But the general climate of the relationship is as I have just portrayed it, and my visit at the beginning of this year confirmed it. It is in this climate that the exceptions have to live and work and do what they can to change things.

Why is the relationship like this? What has happened to Dr. Aziz's prediction in *A Passage to India:** "If it takes five

---

*The exact quotation from Forster's *A Passage to India* reads: "If I don't make you go, Ahmed will, Karim will, if it's fifty-five hundred years we shall get rid of you, yes, we shall drive every blasted Englishman into the sea, and then"— he rode against him furiously—"and then," he concluded, half kissing him, "you and I shall be friends."

hundred years we'll drive every one of you blasted Englishmen into the sea, and then, and then, you and I can be friends." In the event the English were not driven into the sea but took calmly to the boats, and were waved off in a friendly fashion. Why then has Anglo-India survived, in spirit?

Again, there must be many reasons, and the Indians cannot be entirely blameless. To many Western minds they seem volatile, irrational, and unpunctual. A discussion about the weather can sound like the preliminary to murder. The talent they often show for raising a simple arrangement to a level of extreme, incomprehensible complexity is one in which there is a touch of genius—and genius is always irritating. As in any other country, private pockets get lined with public money, but in a poor country like India this seems especially unpalatable. That it is so poor, of course, is no advertisement for one hundred years of direct British rule.

No doubt it is true that there are Indians who will take the visiting experts and official representatives for a ride. But they flatter the English far more often than they fleece them—flatter them unconsciously. The English response to this is not always kind. The level of Indian society with which the British come in contact is so closely modeled on the western British pattern that it lies wide open to British ridicule. The only Englishmen left in the world, Mr. Muggeridge has said, are the Indians. He does not really mean it as a compliment. The Goanese Palm Court orchestra playing "Nights of Gladness" at the Willingdon Club on a Sunday morning, while perfectly dressed and behaved Indians sip their coffee and fruit juices, will very likely bring a smile to the lips of any English there—often a sour smile which says, "Yes, how quaint. *Passé. Déjà vu.* The form but not the style. Nothing is done or ever will be done as well as it used to be."

This notion—widely held I think, seldom openly expressed—is about the only thing that connects the modern Anglo-Indian to thoughts about the old days. The generality of the English in India aren't interested in the imperial past, which is over and done with, and they aren't interested much in India's future because they feel no real commitment to it. They are imprisoned, mostly reluctantly, in their own present. They come for a year or two, and then depart, to be expert somewhere else. There is no commitment beyond the terms of their contracts. And a lot of good intentions can go by the board simply as a result of malaise. To the English, India is an enervating place. You have only to look at the young matrons in the air-conditioned coffee room of Spencer's in Madras, wives of technicians from Stevenage and Luton who seem a bit lost without their prams and cardigans, to know that they wish their husbands' contracts would end soon. *They* are in a state of deep cultural shock. They do not look at the bearers when giving their orders or paying their bills; they hardly look at one another. They are glazed.

When I first saw them I laughed, thought them pretentious little girls trying to act like memsahibs. When I saw them again two weeks later I didn't laugh. I knew that by not looking at the servants they betrayed what else it was they were trying not to see: the poverty outside, the squalor, the filth, the whole shocking ambiance of India encountered for the first time by a woman who not long ago was comfortable chatting to her friends in a New Town supermarket. It was an India for which they did not feel an ounce of responsibility. The empire died almost before they were born.

But in the fortnight's interval I had discovered the ease with which I could go into a state of shock just as deep, perhaps deeper.

For ten days of that fortnight I lived in a village in Andhra Pradesh, in the house of the president of the local village council. It was the only house. The others were mud huts. The village was thirty miles from a railway station. A bus went through once a day. There was no post office, no telephone, no plumbing. It was my stopping-off place between Madras and

Calcutta. I had no official business in the village, no authority, no line of communication, no partner to share my experience, no one from outside who could easily help me if I got into difficulties. As an Englishman, I was quite *alone*.

At first I was quite undisturbed by this. My host was an English-speaking Madrassi, an ex-Havildar who had written to me after the war and with whom I'd kept up a friendly correspondence. The invitation to his village was of long standing. It would have been unthinkable to be within a few hundred miles without going to see him. Indian friends in Madras were concerned for me, so I discovered later, because I hadn't struck them as particularly eccentric.

Memory is kind. I recall the few pleasures more vividly than the miseries, but I don't fool myself that I *felt* my pleasures as keenly as I suffered the miseries. I recall what the miseries were, but mercifully don't *feel* them. I recall walking one morning from the bathing enclosure back to the house, pausing on the mud floor of the compound, shutting my eyes and saying *aloud,* "The whole thing is some awful sort of nightmare."

What I call the Sanders-of-the-river-kick is not really my scene. It might have helped if it had been. I do not like having chairs brought out to me in the middle of the road. I do not like eating alone, food brought in by girls who are pretty but who serve me from behind and run away if I turn round to thank them. I do not like being shaved by a barber on a verandah with a score of people gathered to watch. I do not like being shaved without soap, I do not like my soap rejected without explanation and being left to feel that it is suspected of being unclean from animal fat. I do not like having my forehead and eyelids as well as my beard shaved. The blade might slip. But to all this I submitted, day after day.

I don't mind taking off my shoes and socks and going barefoot all the time I'm in the house, but I do *not* like to see the daughter of the house having to kneel and wash my feet every time I come into the compound. I do not like eating anything

in which the taste of ghee is uppermost, particularly at breakfast, and when my digestive organisms are disturbed—presently
very seriously disturbed. I do not like that, because I don't like
going into a field with a pot of water and no other equipment.
I did that once, because my host obliquely made it clear he
would lose face if his guest did not conform. Fortunately there
was also an ancient disused privy attached to a rice mill, but
this was two hundred yards from the house. One's internal miseries could not be disguised from an observant population. I
made that journey many times a day, with increasing hate in
my heart. The hatred sprang from fear. I was afraid of becoming
desperately ill, of never getting away, of dying in this dreadful
place where I was treated like an animal. The fear became irrational. *Was* I being treated like a king? Wasn't I a *prisoner*?
Was the indignity I was being subjected to a payment back for
some real or imaginary wrong I'd done this man when I was in
a position of authority over him? Why hadn't I met his wife
yet? Surely *that* was a clear sign that he didn't look upon me as
a friend? I became deeply suspicious of him and of the whole
setup.

I became reluctant to go out. I wrote letters. I read old
letters over and over again. I became emotionally attached to
my own luggage, as though it were a fetish. Everything that
reminded me I was English became precious. And gradually I
felt a sahib's face superimpose itself on my own—as I thought—
mild and liberal one. I did not merely accept the chairs of honor,
I expected them. When crossed in a desire I began to raise my
voice, began to give him a hard time.

And yet you see, every day there was a fresh flower on the
table at every meal, every day some mark of affectionate curiosity in this extraordinary stranger. Every day six children trooped
into the room to be helped with their English. I was aware of
all this, but it began to mean *nothing* to me. I longed to see
another white face, and to get back into my own white skin.
And I thought I never would.

On the tenth day, on parting, his wife made her appearance. I thanked her for her kindness and hospitality. She said nothing, looked down at her feet, and I cursed the humility of this Indian woman, knowing that behind locked doors she ruled the roost and would probably have the whole house fumigated after I'd gone. I arrived in Hyderabad next morning, still stunned and vicious. I knocked the hand of a beggar woman off my arm, gave the tonga wallah less than he asked for, ignored his protests and stalked into the Ritz Palace, called for beer and complained about the price. And then sat down in the blessed privacy of a civilized bedroom, with bathroom attached—blessed, blessed bathroom with all mod cons.

My relief was indescribable. But already in that relief there was a shadow of something that appalled me—the growing shadow of my ingratitude, my ridiculous irrational fears, my utter dependence upon the amenities of my own kind of civilization. But the sense of relief was enough to keep the shadow at bay, for a while. So there I was, there *he* is, if you will picture him; sitting on a comfortable bed—Enoch Sahib: a slight case of cultural shock.

And, of course, there—metaphorically—he might have stayed forever, safe and secure, comforting himself that he had learned his lesson, had seen the divergence between the facts of life and his aspirations and insuring himself against a repetition of that disagreeable experience by throwing his aspirations out and rearranging his life to fit the facts, which seems to be the policy advocated by Mr. Powell—a policy advocated in what he calls the national interest.

But this Enoch Sahib did not go on sitting comfortable. He became thoroughly ashamed of himself. His reactions had been understandable, but that did not make them *right*. If they were right, then clearly he should have gone home, closed the gate, shut the door, and never ventured out again. And if *he* would have been right to do that, *we* must obviously all do the same. And then when we are all staring at each other from behind our own familiar kind of prison bars, we shall presumably have the satisfaction of knowing *at least* what this manifest national interest is. The Right Honorable Member for Wolverhampton South-West does not actually say, and so if he has misjudged, by then it might be too late.

He's not awfully good at saying things for himself, although very good at reporting what the large majority are thinking and feeling. When he attempts a synthesis he sometimes comes up with passages that can be turned against him.

It is notoriously a dangerous thing when a country's words and deeds fall out of line with the realities of the world in which that country has to live. It is equally dangerous when the words and deeds of a country's politicians fall out of line with the real sentiments and opinions of that country's people.

Indeed it can be. And personally I'm far from convinced that these people, for whom Mr. Powell has appointed himself spokesman, as yet form a large majority, or that his policy of noninvolvement with international human problems which concern us all because their solutions will affect us all, reflects the real sentiments and opinions *of* the majority. In 1939 I bought a little book of poems by an aspiring young poet, called Enoch Powell—the same man, of course. This is my favorite:

> The autumn leaves that strew the grass
> The flocks of *migrant* birds
> They all are poems, but alas,
> I cannot find the words.

Perhaps there are very many people, who on *serious* reflection, feel as I do, that it is a pity Mr. Powell has since become articulate.

The indifference and noncommitment I detected in many

members of the modern, shifting, Anglo-Indian community are one thing—and perhaps I've helped a bit to explain it and excuse it. But to *encourage* indifference and noncommitment is something else. It is stupid, and therefore dangerous. Its stupidity is often revealed by the nonsense of the arguments offered, for instance, this:

> A widespread fallacy is to notice that rich countries have fine hospitals and universities and expensive elaborate public services and to assume that therefore if one makes a country a present of these things it will be enabled to become rich.

Surely no such fallacy exists, because no one in his right mind has ever thought of international aid in such ludicrous terms. Aid is given because a country is too poor to afford what it is thought right that it should have. Very often its poverty is *partly* explained by our past imperial possession of it. But aid should not be looked on as conscience money. True, aid is seen as an investment in political stability, in friendship instead of enmity. But more than that, I think there must be many ordinary decent Englishmen—to borrow Mr. Powell's emotive phrase—who, *in spite* of the national tendency to insularity, see aid as a means of putting into practice a theory I and they would hate to see disappear from the range of human theories— the theory that it is right for every nation to share, on as equitable a basis as possible, and as soon as possible, all those philosophies, discoveries, developments, and amenities that raise the standards by which the world may live. And not least among those standards are those which we call moral. It is, I believe, *those* standards which Mr. Powell's activities threaten to lower.

THE YORKSHIRE
POST FICTION
AWARD

♦

[This essay was Scott's brief, informal response on December 22, 1971, to receiving the Yorkshire Post Fiction Award *for* The Towers of Silence, *the third volume of* The Raj Quartet. *As part of his gracious acceptance, Scott pokes fun at the way in which scholars, even in their computer analysis of authors, point out at length the obvious and the irrelevant. Scott also pleads for sustaining mystery in writing and expresses his enduring pleasure at the task of creating joy for readers.]*

Scarborough Story. I am glad to be in Scarborough. I've never been in Scarborough before. I've always wanted to come to Scarborough—in fact, since the age of four and a half. I know I was four and a half because when my brother was seven he came to Scarborough alone to visit a friend of the family called Laughton, which may not be a name I should mention in this establishment.

Paul: "I want to go to Scarborough too."
Father: "And so you shall. You will go to Scarborough when you are older."

How right he was. But then he was a Yorkshireman. He was born in Headingley. He went down to London in the first de-

139

cade of the twentieth century. He never came back, but remained a good Yorkshireman. I know he remained a good Yorkshireman because in the summer of his death, 1958, if Yorkshire County lost a match, according to him they were not beaten. They had been Robbed of Victory.

It would please him, I think, to see me here today, a guest of the *Yorkshire Post*, although it's probably a good thing he's not here himself. He became very deaf. If he were here, this is just about the moment he would choose to cup his ear, turn to his neighbor, and say in that loud, carrying voice which deaf people use as a sort of compensation for feeling out of things: "What's the lad saying?"

And that is always a problem. Writing is the loneliest profession. One is flattered to be invited anywhere. One accepts with alacrity. One repents at leisure, facing up to the problem of what to say. In this case I asked my publisher. He replied as follows: "What people like to hear is what made you write the book, and in the case of *The Jewel in the Crown* I think you could provide a fascinating description of your passion for India."

And that seemed to be a good idea, until I remembered that while I feel passion easily enough and have seldom found environment or circumstances an obstacle to feeling it, I have never found it easy to convey to others from a standing position. At least, not so many at a time.

It also seemed to me, on reflection, that while my publisher was probably quite right—that people do like to know what caused a novel to be written—this is not a question the novelist himself need answer. There are always plenty of people only too willing to answer for him. Indeed, things have got to the stage where such people can not only explain why the novel was written but also show cause how the way in which it was written was the wrong way.

Let's take poor Joseph Conrad. It can't have escaped your notice that the interests of English literature were recently considerably served by the discovery that Lord Jim was really a man called Augustus Podmore Williams. Two long studies were published to prove this, and to prove that Conrad really had been out East. It is, you know, not enough to conjure up images of a place which other people familiar with it will immediately recognize as absolutely authentic. Research for these two studies occupied their authors for periods of time well in excess of the time Conrad took to write the novel. Newspaper files going back to the 1880s were turned up, people interviewed, trips made, correspondence conducted on an international scale. So deeply did one of these authors become involved in his investigations that when he realized that Conrad's Lord Jim stayed in Singapore for about a year and the real Lord Jim for nearly forty, he made this comment: "I think this is an instance of Conrad not entirely adapting his source to the fictional character." I find that remarkable. Please note, too, the pedagogic "I think." I find even more remarkable the following comment by the same gentleman: "Sometimes the changes Conrad makes when turning his experiences into fiction are difficult to account for, unless one puts them down to a lapse of memory."

The appearance of these two studies was of course enlivened by angry correspondence in the *Times Literary Supplement* about which of the two authors could rightfully claim the identification of Lord Jim as his own discovery. How it would have amused Conrad. It is not supposed to amuse us. We are supposed to take it terribly seriously. I believe it is supposed to be a way of providing a novelist with credentials, of proving that he was a serious person who did his best to keep his imagination in check and his powers of observation nicely harnessed to a world of recognizable reality. What is particularly funny about these Lord Jim investigations is that only twenty years separated its publication from the notorious and scandalous event on which its main incident was based. But so short is the public memory for its history that no one seems to have noticed it at the time. Another twenty years had to pass before Sir Frank Swettenham wrote to the *Times Literary Supplement* pointing the connection out. Conrad was still alive. But no one seems to have recorded any comment he might have made about what to him must have looked like a late discovery of the always obvious.

This academic third degree, however, is nothing to what we seem to be in for now—the Critical Computer—a machine at present working to show that a novelist didn't write his novel at all. The rumor is circulating that James Bond may not have worked single-handed. The challenge to his reputation comes from no mere mortal but from a computer, one of the biggest and most powerful ever built. A detailed analysis has been carried out by GOVERNMENT SCIENTISTS. . . . Their results suggest that some of the exploits of the master agent were recorded by an author other than Fleming.

In their examination of the Fleming novels they are studying a method used to analyze authorship. Applying the same analysis to other writers, the scientists found that the authorship of books by Graham Greene and G. K. Chesterton might, according to the experiment, also be queried. The method of analysis is straightforward. Several passages of each book are fed into the machine. The computer checks the number of key words such as "and" or "that" in a given length of prose. It automatically analyzes the sentence lengths.

Other novels examined by this method showed even greater variation than those of Ian Fleming. How far these differences can be used to comment on authorship is open to question, the team say. But they have found their studies so fascinating that work will be continued in greater depth.

Before they bother to feed any of my novels in, I assure all whom it may concern that they are the work of only one hand, mine, and that any variations detected are the result of constant attention to the business of trying to write better and to write a different book each time.

I do have one question. For what purpose—in heaven's name—is a team of government scientists analyzing *novels*? It sounds very sinister to me. Surely we have nothing to teach Whitehall about the Craft of Fiction? Can it be that this is a barefaced confession of brotherhood with us? Or is it the sinister thin end of a wedge to be driven by scientists and a certain kind of academic between us and our readers, because they can't bear to accept the fact that—analyze it how they will—in a novel that is any good there will remain a splendid and defiant element of mystery?

Novelists accept that. So do readers. We know that a novel is all lies. That a novel is fun. It is a box of tricks. The only serious thing about a novel is the seriousness with which the writing of it is undertaken. Novelists are really the purveyors of a harmless but exciting addictive drug that heightens the perceptions.

Let us be clear about it. How much of Lord Jim actually happened couldn't matter less. That the book happened is a kind of joy to us. It's the word *joy* I want to emphasize. Next time you're in a bookshop or a library, look round at the faces of your fellow browsers. Not a smile to be seen. It's all wrong. It's not that you don't feel like smiling; it's that you're afraid to.

The atmosphere of ghastly seriousness that surrounds literature also surrounds us. It's the kind of atmosphere in which the literary bodysnatchers flourish. These are the sort of people who try to prove that the novel is dead, because they want it to be. They will take away our pleasure if they can, by persuading us that it's not pleasure but penance—a mixture of social duty and intellectual obligation. *Well, if the novel is dead, all I can say is that it's having a lovely funeral.*

Reading and writing a novel is, in my opinion, a marvelous adventure. Of course it can also be a grubby escapade. But that sort of writer and that sort of reader—so far as I'm concerned— can be thrown to the computer so that it can perform its obvious function of *analyzing instant trash.*

This is, people say, an "instant age." Instant coffee, instant love, instant success, instant wisdom, and instant stupidity. I suppose there is such a thing as instant joy, but that's not the kind I have in mind, which burns much slower. This joy springs from the heightened perception of time and place and people and history—and of oneself revealed mysteriously in an extraordinary and compelling relationship to those things, the kind of relationship Emerson defined as "existing between the hours of our life and the centuries of time," one that remedies the defect of our too-great nearness to ourselves. It is neither an instant joy nor a selfish joy. It establishes itself slowly and lingers a long time afterward. It is the novelist's pleasure to attempt to create it. And it is his privilege to share it.

Thank you.

AFTER MARABAR:
BRITAIN AND INDIA,
A POST-FORSTERIAN VIEW

◆

[From January 29 to February 26, 1972, Scott undertook a stren-
uous lecture tour of India for the British Council as part of the
International Book Year. Traveling without Mrs. Avery-Scott, he
flew to Bombay, then went on to Poona, Baroda, Ahmadābād,
Jaipur, Delhi, Chandīgarh, Calcutta, Rānchī, Madras, Mysore, and
Bangalore. During this time, he spoke mainly to university audiences, both undergraduate and postgraduate, but he also spoke to
more general audiences, such as the Rotary in Bombay. Scott prepared three lectures to deliver on this tour: "After Marabar: Britain
and India, a Post-Forsterian View," "Literature and the Social
Conscience: the Novel," and "The Form and Function of the
Novel." The text of his first lecture comprises a major revision of
his "India: A Post-Forsterian View," given to the Fellows of the
Royal Society of Literature, London, on December 5, 1968. (See
Essays by Divers Hands, ed. Mary Stocks, n.s., vol. xxxvi [Lon-
don: Oxford University Press, 1970], pp. 113–132.) A majority
of Scott's text is changed here and depends less on a close comparison with E. M. Forster's A Passage to India than the earlier
version, and more on commentary about British–Indian history since
Forster's time. Scott takes the occasion to discuss a move in attitude
from the imperial confidence of Forster's time to the state of uncertainty which Scott believed existed from the end of World War II.
He uses Forster's work, for which he expresses admiration, to pro-

vide some terms of contrast with his own. For instance, Forster's Turtons and Burtons are characters primarily taking up stances, but Scott's Turtons regard their work first and their prejudices second. Scott's Turtons exist not in Edwardian sunshine, but in the melancholy of exile; they know those moments of sunlight to be illusory. Further, in contemporary times, Scott hopes that a modern Fielding and a modern Aziz, unlike those two men at the close of Forster's novel, can be friends. Scott sees these contrasts between Forster's time and his own as heightening a changing national ethos that led to the end of the raj.]

The title of this lecture, "After Marabar: Britain and India, a Post-Forsterian View," is one I originally proposed back in November in London, when asked to give some idea of what I could talk about when I got here. It sprang easily to mind, because three years before I had lectured on the subject to the Royal Society of Literature and it seemed a good idea to revise and refurbish my text for an Indian audience; revise—not to tone anything up or down in the cause of good public relations—but because one's ideas, or one's way of expressing them, change, and I knew that when I referred to the text there would be a lot in it which didn't satisfy me.

This proved to be so. I saw that the whole thing would have to be completely rewritten, but before that I had to ask myself whether there was much point. The answer I came up with— and I still don't know whether it provides a proper excuse for exploring the subject further, here—is that in that original text I came closer than I had ever done before to discussing my own work, and to explaining why so much of that work has been about the British–Indian relationship during the days of imperialism in decline. And then I thought that, after all, people in India might like to hear about that, because there—at home— the subject of this relationship has never aroused much thoughtful interest except among those who knew or know India, and they, of course, tend to have views about it which—quite properly—

do not always correspond with mine. For the rest, it is fairly safe to say that, in terms of fiction, the subject is thought to have been dealt with satisfactorily enough by the late E. M. Forster, in his novel *A Passage to India*. And, as you may have noticed, if an Englishman thinks something satisfactory to himself, he often tends to think it satisfactory for everyone.

However, I had committed myself, and on reflection was content to have done so. Apart from earlier books I wrote which had an Indian background, I had spent the last eight years, since a visit in 1964, writing what has turned out to be a sequence of four novels, as yet unfinished, all about this very thing, and although a writer is probably the last person to go to for an explanation of his work, I felt that if I could not say anything about the reasons *why* I write what I do, then there might—I do not say must—be something wrong with me.

There was, though, yet another cause for doubt. I recalled two incidents that took place during my last visit, in 1969. The first concerned an Englishwoman who was asked by a mutual friend, an Indian, what she thought of the first two novels in this quartet about the last days of the British raj. "I suppose they are all right in their way," she said, "but why does he have to revive all that old bitterness?"

The second incident involved an Indian who asked me, "As an Englishman, tell me, what do you think you have to offer the world *today* that might be of value?" This seemed to me such a difficult question that, with that cautious aplomb for which the English are famous, I asked for time to think it over. Three days later when we met, I gave my answer. I said that after mature consideration I thought that the most valuable thing I or someone like me had to offer the world, as an Englishman, was the uncertainty of having anything of value to offer at all.

"In that case," he said, "if they all think like you, the answer is clearly nothing." We remained friends, in fact became rather closer, and four weeks later had a bibulous farewell lunch at the Taj Mahal Hotel in Bombay.

What I meant, of course, was that if your country happens to be one with a long historical record of believing that it knows best about everything, one that has imposed its will, exerted its power, and extended its influence over very many areas of the world for very many years, in the bland conclusion that even if other countries didn't like it, it was good for them just the same—then, when the time comes, as of course it must, when doubts about the morality of this situation has spread, when the assumption of superiority has been subjected to the withering fire of self-criticism, adverse opinion, and active opposition, and the whole tottering edifice has finally been handed over to the monuments commission as an interesting relic of that country's history—then the very last thing one wants to feel is that the whole process of imposing one's national personality on other people is starting again on a subtler and perhaps more insidious level.

I think what my friend had expected when he asked the question was a reply that subtly gave away one's feeling that one was not only valuable but unique—a reply, in fact, in an apologetic English mumble in which the only audible words would have been "integrity" and "moral leadership," and he would probably and quite properly have pounced on these and forced me to admit I couldn't justify them. In fact, I think he was really playing a game with me, but he had asked the question. And recollecting it, coupling it with that lady's comment, "Why does he have to revive all the old bitterness?" it seemed to me for a moment that there I was, about to come out of India, not sure that I had anything of value to offer except being unsure I had anything, and at the same time open to a charge of reviving memories best forgotten.

The path that leads from the desert of uncertainty back only to the well of bitterness seems a bad one to take and, as a novelist, a poor one to have mapped out. But I have in mind a more positive and useful geography. And it is this geography that I must try to throw some light on—let us call it a sidelight

148

because the direct light, if it exists, is there in the novels—but in any case I must do so without refuting that charge about reviving bitterness and certainly standing by what I said about the most valuable thing I felt I had to offer, as an Englishman, being my uncertainty about having anything at all, because that describes to me what even an *English* novelist is. To me the novel, among other things, is a form of moral dialogue between the writer and the reader. It is much more a series of questions than a set of statements. It invites from the reader not dumb acquiescence but a creative and critical response to the life it depicts. A novel cannot effectively be built on dogma. However self-assured, even opinionated, it may seem, however deeply it lulls the reader, however unprotestingly the reader is borne along by it, in the end it makes the same kind of statement/question which that controversial English critic, F. R. Leavis, sees as definitive of the nature of criticism. "This is so, isn't it?" To which Dr. Leavis requires, I think properly, the response, "Yes, but . . ."

Both the question and the answer are hedged about by uncertainty. Without such uncertainty, it seems to me, society can only be static, and without the freedom to express its uncertainty, a society will finally be oppressive. In the heat of the moment, or merely to pass the time pleasantly in company, one will make dogmatic statements that appear to admit of no argument. But that is one thing. In one's heart there must always be, I think, the murmur of a doubt about any position one may have taken up. And the human heart, especially, is within the novelist's province. He must detect and record the murmur, as well as he can. He cannot do much better than listen attentively to his own.

Sometimes I am asked why—as an Englishman living in the latter half of the twentieth century—I spend so much of my time writing books about the last days of imperial India. Surely, such people say, the novelist's job is to illustrate the world he lives in now, but anything *you* write about is over—over for the

English, for the Indians, for the world. It has been settled; it no longer matters. One or two critics say this too, and perhaps more feel it without bringing themselves to say it, at least in print. And as I get older, and the critics get younger—a strange phenomenon which most creative people become familiar with—as imperial India recedes further and further and is therefore seen to have been more and more satisfactorily dealt with by E. M. Forster, and as these young critics begin to notice that in my books many of the English characters are sympathetically portrayed, the suspicion occasionally arises—at home—that I am an imperialist-manqué, vicariously regretting the joys of the punkah, which they think is a drink. One such young man dismissed the second novel in *The Quartet* as "so much north-west frontier flag-wagging, for moderns." It was an isolated opinion but it marked significantly, the tendency there is in every generation to see only what it wants to see, or thinks it ought to see. That young man obviously had a view—a received one—of British India. If he *had* to read a book about it he wanted the view confirmed. He was looking for dogma, in effect for mere repetition. When he didn't get it he ignored all the passages that could by no stretch of the imagination have been called north-west frontier flag-wagging for moderns, and presumably concentrated with tremendous disapproval on those parts of the novel that tried to deal, justly, through one or two British characters, with the genuine affection for India and grief at awareness of its imminent loss in their working lives that in actual life characterized perhaps not a few of them.

But there it is, the question asked—Why don't I write books that illustrate the world I live in, the world from which imperial India has disappeared? The neatest answer I can give is that in my opinion, I have done and I do. Neatness, however, is all very well. The truth is, as usual, untidier.

Another English critic, Walter Allen, has very usefully defined the novel as "an extended metaphor of an author's view of life." At once we have got the priorities better arranged, with that prominence given not to "the world" but to the "author's view," and have properly substituted "life" for "the world."

So that my proper answer to the question, "Why do you, as a modern English novelist of serious pretentions, bother to write about the time-expired subject of the British raj?"—and that is what is implied—is, must be, if my novels are novels at all, "Because the last days of the British raj are the metaphor I have presently chosen to illustrate my view of life."

But before the smile of satisfaction at having apparently dealt effectively with the question has quite formed, I know that I am in trouble again. I can ask the next question myself all too easily and find it all to difficult to answer—the question, "What *is* your view of life and how does the metaphor you have chosen illustrate it?"

You understand the problem. Or will in a moment. If I now came down into the audience and dragged one of you up to the platform and said, "Tell me, tell us all, your view of life," that unfortunate man or woman would in all likelihood be in some doubt whether he, or she, *had* a view of it except that it was full of unpleasant surprises.

I, of course, am forewarned and forearmed, but that doesn't help much. Life is so complex that one's view of it is inevitably diffuse. The eye wanders across the vast panorama and occasionally pauses and intensifies its focus. Behind this kind of selectivity is an emotion not easily isolated or indexed.

But one likely way a novelist has of checking up on his view is to summarize, quite barely, what his novels have been about, in order to see whether a common factor emerges.

My first was about the difficulty one officer had, in India during the war, taking over another officer's job. The second was about an Englishman to whom Indian independence meant losing a job he loved. The third was about a man back home in London from the East, too ill from tropical disease to do a proper job and feel he had a stake in the future. The fourth was about a soldier in India who was obsessed by the idea that men had died because he hadn't done his job properly and that his job now was to bring out in a younger man those qualities he lacked himself but thought important. The fifth was a bit of a hybrid, but the job motif recurs in a theme of madness brought on by obsession with occupations for their own sake—occupations disrupted or invented by war. The sixth was about a man who spent his childhood in India and returned there, taking a sabbatical year from his London office because he hated the feeling that he had become no more than a consumer of things made by other people. Two non-Indian books followed—the first a comedy of London life in the 1960s, its middle-aged hero a man ruined by a small inheritance which had been just big enough to make doing a job seem like something he could do tomorrow. He was a consumer too, especially of gin. The next, the eighth I had written, was narrated by an elderly writer who lived in Spain with a beautiful wife and an unfinished manuscript, both of which were unfaithful to him.

It was only then, after the eighth novel and a visit to India in 1964, that I turned actively to the history of Britain in India. In the eight previous novels, the common factor that emerges clearly is this obsession with the relationship between a man and the work he does. I'd think of it as puritan had not Stendhal of all people once written, "Without work the vessel of life has no ballast."

Puritan or not, it would seem to be an obsession, and from the number of times that India—British India—has been chosen as the background to the events described, one may say that British India was an obsession too, so that it appears that one has a double obsession—an obsession with British India and an obsession with the importance to the main characters of their work.

If there is a common connection perhaps it isn't clear, at least not in regard to work. In British India, surely, the sahib was shaved while he still slept, then led, stupefied, to the gusl-khana [bath], folded into his tin tub, doused, dried, powdered,

152

dressed; creakily mounted on a no-less creaky pony and precariously pointed in the direction of the daftar. Arriving there with sleep receding and temper rising, he would dock his clerk a week's pay for losing a file, order four peasants out of his sight, three fined, two rigorously imprisoned, and one to District and Sessions for deportation; and then address himself to the more agreeable business of writing a sharp minute to the divisional commissioner about the civil engineer's plan to drain the marsh out at Mudpore for a scheme that might certainly improve agricultural conditions but would more certainly and more importantly drive out the duck and ruin the shooting. Thus kindled, he would return to his bungalow, riding his pony to a lather of terminal fever, kick the syce in the seat of his pants for not catching him as the loyal beast fell dead at the foot of the bungalow steps, then stump up to the veranda in full view of the whole vast retinue of his servants, but shouting "Koi Hai" ["Is anyone there?"] in response to some deep reflexive notion of the protocol to be observed, then clatter into the dark, polished dining room and sit at the end of the long, dark, polished table, where for a moment he would be puzzled by the presence of a woman of deprived aspect reading letters at the other end of it. Then, remembering it was memsahib, he would mutter, "Hullo, old thing," and bury himself behind the pages of the *Civil and Military Gazette*.

Not much obsession with work there. But I suggest all that can be dismissed as caricature. And perhaps we can dismiss obsession from the argument and again use the word metaphor instead, and say that the recurring theme of men at work or not at work but wanting to be, in British India or elsewhere, is used as a metaphor to convey a view of the life we live nowadays, anyway in the West, as one that seems to offer few rewards to the man or woman who feels he must do work of some positive value, not in the context of society as such—there are plenty of positive opportunities there—but in the context of the philosophy on which that society bases its aspirations.

153

It is here, in the metaphor, that the real obsession is disclosed. An obsession not with the importance of work to man, but with the idea that while love, as T. S. Eliot said, is most nearly itself when here and now cease to matter, life is most nearly itself when here and now not only matter much but can be felt to matter; when here and now are governed by a philosophy in pursuit of whose truths and rewards men know they can honorably employ themselves. A story about men deeply involved in, obsessed by, their occupations is an extended metaphor of that idea. A story about men at work in British India is the same metaphor, particularized. But that is rather more difficult to provide credentials for, because the suspicion must immediately arise that to write about British India is to express regret for a here and now that mattered and has been lost. Which would seem, certainly, to make me an imperialist-manqué, yearning for Poona and the punkah.

The truth is quite otherwise, and I suppose that lady who accused me of reviving "all that old bitterness' is a witness in my defense, since bitterness of the kind she meant is scarcely the flavor to be expected from works rooted in regret for a lost utopia. Rooted in anger perhaps, but above all, I hope, in as accurate a portrayal as I can manage of the time and circumstances that caused bitterness to flow on both sides. Bitterness, yes, but other things too, which she did not mention.

I am the sort of person who thinks that the philosopher, Emerson, was right when he said, "Man is explicable by nothing less than all his history." Indeed, I made sure that Barbara Batchelor, a retired English missionary and an imaginary character in the third novel in the quartet, *The Towers of Silence*, should find the essay by Emerson in which this thing is said, when browsing among the volumes on the shelves of the club subscription library, in a place called Pankot in 1942, and be duly impressed by it. And I see now that her tin trunk of missionary relics, which gives her so much trouble throughout the book, but to which she is loyal, even more loyal to it than to her God, who seems unfairly to have deserted her, is really a symbol for the luggage I am conscious of carrying with me every day of my life—the luggage of my past, of my personal history and of my country's history and of the world's history; luggage crammed with relics of achievement, of failure, of continuing aspirations and optimistic expectations. One is not ruled by the past, one does not rule or reorder it, one simply *is* it, in the same way that one is as well the present and part of the future. It sounds and is pretty exhausting. The one thing one cannot escape in life is its continuity. Perhaps one feels this most strongly in middle age and after. Again to quote T. S. Eliot—whom, in middle age, I begin to recognize as perhaps the greatest literary influence on my life, although no one exerts an influence unless there is already a correspondence of outlook for the influence to work upon—to quote Eliot:

> Home is where one starts from. As we grow older
> The world becomes stranger, the pattern more complicated
> Of dead and living. Not the intense moment
> Isolated, with no before and after,
> But a lifetime burning in every moment
> And not the lifetime of one man only
> But of old stones that cannot be deciphered.

And yet again, as Emerson—another American, dash it— as Emerson put it in his essay on history, "Each new law and political movement has meaning for you. Stand before each of its tablets and say 'Here is one of my coverings. Under this fantastic, or odious, or graceful mask did my Proteus nature hide itself.' This remedies the defect of our too-great nearness to ourselves."

If I believe this, as I do, then obviously I believe in forgiving but not in forgetting. To forget strikes me as the quickest way of making the same mistake again, and perhaps the fear of the consequences of forgetting lies solidly behind the work I do. I'm not sure that there is genuinely any such thing as for-getting, but there are tender conspiracies of silence, and these may engender ignorance, always a dangerous thing.

May I attempt now an explanation of my affection for this country?—I think we have reached that stage—and I say "at-tempt" because if it is necessary to explain it, I cannot really do so any more than I can explain why one should acquire an affection for, or fall in love with, one person instead of an-other. At the bottom of personal affections there must, I sup-pose, be some kind of mutual recognition, but how a country can recognize a person I simply don't know. One finds oneself, in that territory, thrashing about in the lush regions of the pa-thetic fallacy.

Nevertheless it was in the first place the country, because in the early 1940s, when I first came here, one did not, as an English soldier, easily meet many of the indigenous population or become what would be described as intimate. On the other hand, I believe that the topography and physical actuality of a country impose something of their character upon the people to whom it belongs—and perhaps eventually upon those who visit it. So you may say, if you like, that I approached you first through the lie of your land and the way the light falls on it.

I can't say that my affections were immediately aroused, be-cause the first thing that happened to me was jaundice, and that is not the ideal basis on which to begin an affair of any kind. But I think they were aroused more strongly than I had time to recognize, because about fourteen years ago I wrote the following passage describing a young soldier's reaction to his first Indian billet, and I don't think I could have written it, after the event, in just this way if I had not, however subcon-sciously, felt it at the time.

Behind the hut was a stretch of rough, uncut grass. Bushes formed a hedge. The hill sloped away from the hedge, and its trough could not be seen. But, beyond, the land lay in folds covered in grass of a green which Ramsay now knew was a green he did not know because a fiercer rain, a stronger sun, a drier dust, had stained its pigment. He stood in the doorway of his and Lawson's hut and saw that the sky had no colour he recognized and that the shape of the land was not a shape which he understood in his bones. He became aware of a scent in which there was mixed the smoke from fires he had not seen and the tang of earth he had not touched; and when the breezes moved there was in it the breath of men he had not met; and his blood stirred.

Like Ramsay, I had not wanted to come out here, I was sent; and, like Ramsay, my ignorance was immense, as great as my disappointment at finding it, when I arrived, raining. In my ignorance of the place, the people, and the history, I was representative not just of Ramsay but of many of my countrymen, who in the main had for years been under the misapprehension that the uttermost point unattainable—ultimate truth—lay midway between Dover and Calais, and that everything beyond was bad news. In my belief that India was bad news, bad news in my case because I knew we ought not to have it but jolly well give it back—a belief that was part of the package deal of a youthful liberal humanism at that time largely uncorrupted by vicissitudes—I was representative of a smaller but still sizable body of public opinion at home. But the basic factor of my response was ignorance.

It has seemed to me subsequently that no record of the history of the British–Indian relationship can be complete unless the ignorance of India by a vast majority of the British living on their own island is taken account of. I do not mean ignorance of Indian manners, customs, religions, and domestic arrangements, but ignorance of the way India was acquired, of the way it was administered, and of the way it contributed to the well-being of the people of that island; ignorance of the

157

background to the policies that were pursued from time to time; ignorance of the multiple and conflicting interests that were at stake; and of course ignorance of the many-faceted response of individual Indians to individual Britons and vice versa. And, finally, ignorance of the issues that apparently made it impossible to hand it back in one piece. Broadly, you could say that the British electorate, taken as a whole, was in the anomalous position of exerting influence on a country of which it knew nothing, and often had no way of finding out about, because Indian affairs, except in the broadest possible sense, simply never came up for discussion in domestic electoral programs. But when a party had been voted into office and a ministry was formed to fulfill a mandate, a secretary of state for India was appointed and, by pressures and directives, attempted to put the ignorant electorate's duly expressed opinions into operation in *this* country, where, of course, anything like full parliamentary procedure promptly stopped. That the situation was always understood to be peculiar—perhaps inescapably peculiar—is shown by the fact, and I think this is right, that whenever an Indian question was tabled in the House of Commons the chamber emptied like a shot.

It is an ignorance that still persists, and, while it no longer has the same effect, one of the first fruits of ignorance is prejudice, and so I am sorry that it does. I should like to think that here and there in the books I write there are things which, at home, reduce the weight of ignorance, and consequently of prejudice.

Prejudice is a many-headed dragon. I spoke a moment ago of my youthful liberal humanism, and this prejudiced me in advance against representatives of the imperial power. It takes time to adjust the focus and see that power is exerted in different ways by individuals.

It took time, certainly. On my first arrival, I felt that the English I met who belonged out here were almost unrecognizable as English at all. They seemed preserved in some kind of Edwardian sunlight. Recently I put this thought into the mouth

158

of an imaginary character, a wretched cad of a chap, just out from home, who had designs on the daughter of a colonel in the infantry. The time—1944. He said to her, early in the process of seduction, "Extraordinary, isn't it, that the people in this country who feel most like foreigners to each other are English people who have just arrived and the ones who have been out here for years. It makes me want to say 'Where have you all been? Come back. All is forgiven.' " To which she replies, "Come back where? Forgiven by whom and for what?" A few pages later, I regret to say, she succumbed.

I quote that passage because it maps, as a novelist will map such things, the journey one takes from a particular prejudice to a general uncertainty. The girl in question is not denying that he and she, although both English, are strangers. In fact she feels it quite strongly, and when she asks, "Come back where?" she is conveying something of the melancholy that presently I myself noticed in members of the raj of my day, the melancholy arising from too long an exile, from too far a removal from the source of dynamic native experience, which I suppose people feel they need if they are to share that other sense of having something of approved and proven value to offer as a people to other people. The melancholy, too, of knowing that a principal source of comfort, the continuing support of the people who have sent you out to do a job, has begun to erode. And perhaps above all, the melancholy of knowing that even after twenty, thirty years of living in the country, it has been, still is, exile, because a certain loftiness and detachment have been required or dabbled in or chosen, home has remained home, and India, however long lived in, never been truly identified with.

But to return to that girl (by way of illustration), counter to her melancholy there is—was—a dash of natural spirit, that of someone who cannot feel personally much responsible for what has gone wrong and is going wrong, but who, on the contrary, has tried honorably to perform a task. "Forgiven by whom?" she asks. "And for what?"

All this I would call post-Forsterian. Forster was a very great writer, and A *Passage to India* is a very great novel. My admiration for it has increased on each of the three occasions I've read it, and I've found new things in it on each of them. As my own understanding of the British–Indian past grows, so does my understanding of Forster's British–Indian novel. I see it now as a novel with a powerful prophetic element, as a philosophical novel, not a social novel. I read it for the first time after my return from India, postwar. It was then the social aspect that I saw as central to it, and in that regard I had certain reservations. They weren't strong enough to be pointed to as a source of my own subsequent concerns as a writer about India— in any case one does not write out of one's feelings about books but out of one's feelings about life. But the reservations persisted, grew stronger the more I studied the history of British India and attempted to pass that history through the selecting mechanism of my own experience and recollections.

My reservations concerned both the raj characters and the Indian characters. Forster called his British–Indian characters the Turtons and Burtons, as those of you who have read the book will recall. I think it was the late Gilbert Murray who, commenting on John Galsworthy's Forsytes, said that apart from one thing, they struck him as absolutely right, perfectly recognizable. The one thing that worried him was that, on reflection, he felt he'd never actually met any. I felt something like that about Forster's Turtons and Burtons. Something, not everything. And something similar about an Indian character such as Dr. Aziz—a feeling that grows stronger the more the English actor Peter Sellers and his imitators persist in their comic portrayals of Indian immigrants.

Let us just say that sociologically something seemed to be missing. The explanation wasn't wholly to be found in the fact that A *Passage to India* was a portrait of British India in 1913 and I didn't reach there until 1943. In very many ways there cannot have been a great deal—outwardly—to distinguish the India of 1913 from the one to which I myself first made passage—little, that is to say, to distinguish the British side of British India. And, as I said, it took time to lose that sensation that the English people I met who lived out here were the more foreign to me; more foreign than the Indians whom I met in anterooms and messes, on parade, in the daftar, in shops, railway stations, Indians who did things for me that I was not used to having done (having never employed a personal body servant), Indians who sold things to me, and those comparatively few Indians who were simply my companions, undergoing the same military experience. Because they seemed unself-conscious, a bond of common humanity was much more easily forged between myself and the Indians I met in these ways than between myself and the sahibs and memsahibs, who were always, I thought, conscious of having to represent something—indeed, had I read A Passage to India then, I'm sure I would have thought, "By God, Forster's right," and then perhaps it would have been more difficult for me to read it later and feel—if the book was to be taken as an accurate social record of the India of my own day—that something was missing, or felt that I had never actually met a Turton or a Burton, or for that matter, a Dr. Aziz. Mrs. Moore and Adela Quested were different kettles of fish. They were not old India hands but, like myself, new arrivals. It is interesting to me to note now that the three of us went different ways. Mrs. Moore found the whole situation too difficult. She was too old, too ill to cope with it. She turned her back on it and went home and died on the P & O. Miss Quested found it difficult too, but her response to that was to retreat into the wrathful, protective arms of the Turtons and Burtons. She became, to an extent, one of them. Even Fielding, that liberal-humanist schoolmaster, seems to me to go sour, and although at the end he says to Dr. Aziz, "Why can't we be friends now? It's what I want. It's what you want," Forster ends the book with the passage:

But the horses didn't want it—they swerved apart; the earth didn't want it, sending up rocks through which

161

riders must pass single file; the temples, the tank, the jail, the palace, the birds, the carrion, the Guest House, that came into view as they issued from the gap and saw Mau beneath; they didn't want it, they said in their hundred voices, "No, not yet" and the sky said, "No, not there."

That "No, not there" is a little puzzling. "No, not yet," one can understand, in context, but "No, not there" seems on the face of it to reject the possibility of *ever*, in *India*, if we take the context at its face value, as a context dealing with the question of just when and where Fielding and Aziz can be friends. But taking *A Passage to India* at its face value is not a course to be recommended. Its subtleties are endless, and the fact that, as I hope, a modern Fielding and a modern Aziz can be friends here, friends now, in all probability does not invalidate Forster's meaning.

Neither do my reservations about his Turtons and Burtons invalidate it, for as I have said, according to my modern reading of *Passage*—and I think I only see it this way because my instincts have led me in the same direction—it is not a novel about the nice English allying themselves, or trying to, with the nice Indian against the *nasty* English, but one that foresees a day when both the liberal instinct and reactionary instinct, as we have known them, as Forster knew them, will run out of steam, come up against the rockface of a particular civilization's terminus, which I see as symbolized in the Marabar Caves, where there was that echo that frightened Mrs. Moore. "Boum," it went, and Forster went on to say that "boum," coming at a moment when Mrs. Moore chanced to be fatigued, "had managed to murmur, 'Pathos, piety, courage—they exist but are identical; and so is filth. Everything exists. Nothing has value'— Then she was terrified over an area larger than usual; the universe, never comprehensible to her intellect, offered no repose to her soul . . . and she realised that she didn't want to . . .

162

communicate with anyone, not even with God. She sat motionless with horror." Well—as again Eliot has said—still as we may sit we must be still moving.

Although you couldn't really say for "Mrs. Moore" read "E. M. Forster," since he hardly sat motionless with horror during the many distinguished years he subsequently lived, Marabar was the end of the road for the Forster who wrote novels. And there is an extraordinarily close connection between Mrs. Moore's disagreeable experience of the caves in 1913, created between then and 1924, and the haunting fear of our modern western civilization that indeed everything exists and nothing has value, which is why I call it a prophetic novel.

In the field of literary criticism it is well established that on one level A *Passage to India* is an acting-out of what is called the liberal dilemma, and on that level Forster's position is quite clear. One by one his liberal characters stand up to be counted and then sit down, smothering poor Dr. Aziz in the process. The Turtons remain smugly in command. But it strikes me as a remarkable thing to have forseen that the liberal dilemma— that of proving in the early 1920s in the world of affairs that the liberal idea could work without the use of illiberal force— might lead to the inertia implicit in the phrase "Everything exists, nothing has value," because at that time, and well into my own, the liberal idea, or so it seemed, was slowly making its mark in the world of affairs, it was coming into an ascendency. To me as a youth, there was the liberal idea alone, but no liberal dilemma.

There was, to use a now much-used word, a confrontation between Turtonism and Fieldingism, I don't mean just in British India but to an even greater extent in Britain. The conflict between Turtonism and Fieldingism in India came in a somewhat different form—in that of Indian national opposition to an entrenched foreign authority. Fieldingism at home approved and supported Fieldingism in India. The source of inspiration was the same in both cases—a belief in the essentially dynamic nature of man and the structure of society, as one that required of authority within a framework of law guarantees of individual freedom, social justice, and equal opportunities. But although British Fieldings supported Indian Fieldings, it would be a mistake to say that Indian independence was high on their list of priorities. To them, Indian independence was something that would automatically happen when the confrontation with Turtonism in general was brought to a successful conclusion.

And I should say that this period—say 1920 to approximately 1950—was the last, to date, in British history in which the fire of absolute convictions about the right direction to take, or about a direction being taken having to be opposed (in Spain and Germany for instance), could be felt and seen to burn. The period reached its peak—one might say its apotheosis—in the British postwar elections of 1945. Liberal humanists had perhaps forgotten, or never fully realized, that *uncertainty* about the right direction to take was its root, and that without uncertainty even a liberal-humanistic society would be as static and as finally oppressive as any other.

It has been said that the British, having lost an empire, are still looking for a role, and while there is some truth in that, it is not, I think, the whole truth, or even true about Britain only, except in regard to losing an empire. And in regard to *that*, most of us prefer to think that we didn't lose it but gave it up. For the majority of the British electorate that wasn't very difficult, because if you don't know much about what you have, you don't know what you're handing back. I am very conscious that, in offering "giving up" as a more appropriate term than "losing," I may appear not only to denigrate what was in fact an intense and—as it would have proved—irresistible opposition here in India to being held on to, but also to overlook the fact that when you run out of steam you can't hold on to anything, sometimes not even your wife. I neither intend to denigrate nor to overlook. *British* India *was* running out of steam. There were several contributory factors, chief among them the virtual impossibility of administering a country that had decided it damn well wasn't going to be administered any longer. But steam had also gone out because for years the administration had known that what it stood for was becoming increasingly unpopular at home. In performing where they performed they knew they were no longer completely in tune with the changing national ethos.

That is central to my position as a writer of these novels about the last days of the British raj. My Turtons exist not in perpetual Edwardian sunshine but in the shadows, the melancholy of exile. There are exceptions, but the lighting is thus, the climate so. They realize that they no longer swim boldly on the tide of affairs. The Edwardian sunlight that sometimes still seems to dapple the waters is an illusion, and, by and large, they know it.

And if I may point to another difference between my Turtons and Burtons and Forster's—and I am not making a literary comparison, but one of attitude arising from a view of life more social than philosophical—it is that I attempt to portray them within the context of their *work* first and their prejudices second. In *Passage,* the raj struck me as notably *unoccupied* by anything so much except the need to take up a stance or attitude. As a social novelist rather than a philosophical novelist, I miss in *Passage* references to a concern and belief in occupation which, coupled with the conviction and certainty that the occupation was both created by and in rigid line with the national British ethos, led to the rigidity of attitude. Perhaps in 1913 one should not look for that, or therefore miss it. But I have, in terms even of the social novel, a doubt.

For much the same reason—apart, that is, from the more obvious explanation that I write about a period dating some twenty years later than Forster's, when things had changed on both sides—I have always tried to portray major Indian characters from the same angle, that is to say at work, or trying to be at work—work in which they can believe, or work which doesn't comfort or satisfy them because there is, to put it frankly, a limit of their expectations of reaching the point at which their talents will be fully extended. It is all part of the same view, expressed in the British–Indian metaphor, of the importance to a man, or to a woman, of engaging himself honorably, not in a conflict as conflict, or for conflict's sake, but in work or acts that are not, to put it simply, entirely selfish.

And putting it this way, perhaps one comes closer to what connects us than to what divides us, as human beings. An Indian critic domiciled in England once very kindly complimented me on getting all sorts of different people *right*—a memsahib, a sahib, an Indian politician, an Indian man of letters, a British soldier, an Indian clerk. But when I thought about it—and a novelist does not take much time to think about what he feels, in case he finds himself thinking he ought not to feel it—I decided that I had not really been very clever. Apart from observing things like speech, mannerisms, customs, social attitudes—and in the process probably getting as much wrong as I got right—I realized that in an emotional or psychological fictional situation I've always asked myself, "In this man's or woman's *position* what would I feel?" and the most useful answer has always been, I think, "Perhaps what I would feel myself."

A point I haven't yet taken further is the one about looking for a role. I'm not sure that as a nation one should; the idea is a bit self-regarding. On the whole, I should say the time for roles of the kind that were meant by the man who said that thing—starring roles on the international political scene—has expired or is due to expire, mostly in tragic circumstances, in view of the evidence. I suppose that it's easy enough for an Englishman to say this, because—like Macbeth's poor players—we certainly had our hour to strut and fret. One's uncertainty here about the usefulness, the morality of roles is tempered by one's knowledge of the ease with which, as an Englishman, one might stand accused of sour grapes.

But in any case, there can't be a role for any nation if the

national ethos is not strong, and here again I am not sure that
the time for a purely national ethos hasn't expired too. A national ethos can be very dangerous. But here is a dilemma.
Without it a nation *could* go to pieces. With it that same nation can enslave or destroy others. But this looks like a dilemma that a younger generation than my own must and, I
think, will solve. Meanwhile one can only speak for one's own
generation, on the basis of what one has experienced by living
as part of it, but of course in the hope that if there *is* anything
of value in what one says of what one has learnt, something of
that might linger a bit, hang in the air, and not be entirely
lost.

Once again, as between Britain and India, as between my
own British generation and the Indian generation that corre-
sponds with it, I see more clearly what connects than what
divides. For instance, that there must surely be an emotional
correspondence between our giving you up or losing you and
your kicking us out, or anyway persuading us in the light of
incontrovertible evidence that it was time we went; an emotional correspondence in the shape of a shared moment, possibly a prolonged one, of hiatus, as together we found one kind
of occupation gone and one kind of ideal fulfilled—whichever
way it was, whichever way one chooses, but leaving an emotional vacuum to be filled, and occasions of immediate and
pressing demands on our stores of energy, ingenuity, and ideal-
ism. In neither case can the past be discounted. We have both
inherited it, even if we didn't personally make it. And in many
subtle ways it still connects us. Why should it not? It was a
human experience. Another thing that connects us is the fact
that the world into which we both floated off, as from an aban-
doned imperial shore, was one for which neither of us was fully
prepared, but that was more our fault than yours.

And certainly we share the present. In the books I write
about the last days of British India—whether they are meta-
phors, obsessions, or anything else—I am conscious of this pres-

ent, the one I am living in, leaning its weight on the vanished world I attempt to illustrate, as if it is looking for an extra source of inspiration, so that it is sometimes difficult for me to determine what was then, what is now, and what is yet to be. The best, I hope, as Robert Browning assured us.

LITERATURE AND THE
SOCIAL CONSCIENCE:
THE NOVEL

◆

["Literature and the Social Conscience: The Novel" *is the text of a lecture that Scott delivered several times during his tour of India for the British Council in 1972. Two of the lecture sites were the India International Centre in Delhi and St. Joseph's College, Calicut University. In this essay, Scott explores the relation between an author and society; he speaks to the central importance of the image itself and his interest in the residual element of mystery in his fiction—what he calls life as continuity instead of objectives—by posing those questions that will remain mysteries, not those to which he has the answers. Appropriate to the idea of mystery, Scott closes his essay with a series of questions for his audience to ponder.]*

Shelley described the poet as the unacknowledged legislator of mankind. Lenin called Tolstoy the mirror of the Russian Revolution. Tolstoy said he was influenced by the work of Charles Dickens. So is it to the author of *Hard Times* that the world owed Joseph Stalin? To whom do we owe Dr. Verwoerd? Or Senator McCarthy? Does the man of letters take credit only for progressive legislation and accept no blame for the reactionary?

Perhaps it would have been better if Shelley had called writers the guardians of a sacred flame, but faced with the choice of being an administrator or a vestal virgin, which of us would choose the latter? On the whole I can't help wishing Shelley had kept his mouth shut. I feel it may be to him we owe that awful word *commitment,* and Sartre's word *engagement,* which means discovering and working within your unique historical situation.

In a recent book called *The Writer and Commitment,* the author, Mr. John Mander, says:

> All art is committed, it would seem, to something beyond itself, to a statement of value not purely aesthetic, to an Arnoldian "criticism of life." But the fear of politics remains. Our insistence that commitment is neither left-wing nor exclusively political in connotation may serve to allay certain misapprehensions. But it has still to be shown that the term is just and necessary—that it is meaningful to ask of a writer: To what is he in the last resort committed?

I quote this passage because the question "To what is the writer in *the last resort* committed?" is also meaningful to this talk, in which I ought perhaps to warn you I shall discuss the novel as a work of art, as a creative work in the medium of prose, and not as a poor journalistic relation of poetry.

When Tolstoy was twenty-four he said, "Literature is rubbish. I should like to set down rules and a plan of estate management." When he was seventy, he said, "Art is human activity, and therefore its value must be weighed in proportion as art is serviceable or harmful to mankind. It must be accessible and comprehensible to everyone."

Two years later he wrote his last major work, *Resurrection.* He wrote it to raise money in aid of a religious sect that was being persecuted. *Resurrection* was certainly accessible and comprehensible, and it was serviceable to mankind because it made a lot of money for the czar's victims, who emigrated to Canada. It was published in 1899. In that same year Henry James, also an elderly man, began the four-year stint that produced *The*

Ambassadors, The Wings of a Dove, and *The Golden Bowl.* Could two men be less alike in their approach to the novel? Was one approach right and the other wrong?

I hope I'm not expected to form a judgment for anyone but myself. There is a story—isn't there?—of a man of letters who was invited to address an audience on the subject of creative writing. Reaching the rostrum after the usual gratifying preliminaries with members of the faculty, he enquired how many of the people gathered there intended to become creative writers. Nearly every hand rose.

"Then why are you sitting here?" he asked. "Go home and get on with it."

I hasten to say that in this case it is not *your* presence in this room that I cast doubts on, but my own. As a practicing novelist I write novels in order to find out, among other things, what they are, and not to explain what they should be. And so, although as I grow older it seems to me that the critics grow younger, perhaps it is to critics one has to look for definitions and for anything like an objective investigation into literature and the social conscience.

Let us look to one now—Mr. Cyril Connolly, who wrote a book in 1938 called *Enemies of Promise.* The threatened "promise" of the title was literary promise, and its enemies, according to Mr. Connolly, were politics, conversation, drink, casual sex, journalism, and worldly success. I am threatened by several of these, which I shall significantly fail to enumerate. And if it should seem that Mr. Connolly has plumped against legislation in favor of virginity, I should point out that he doesn't ask the writer totally to abstain but to partake, as Henry James would have said, with, as it were, caution.

Connolly wrote *Enemies of Promise* as an inquiry into the problem of how to write a book that lasts ten years. It has lasted twenty-five already, so Mr. Connolly clearly knew what he was talking about. He is certainly more encouraging in his definitions than Tolstoy. "Literature," Mr. Connolly says, "is the art of writing something that will be read twice."

He does not say by whom. An aunt of mine read *Rebecca* no less than nine times to my knowledge. What he means, of course—and in other parts of the book says so—is that literataure is work that keeps, that survives either the shock of being fashionable or the indignity of being overlooked when it first appears. The survival need not appear to be continuous. A book's appeal can wax and wane like a moon. Like a moon, it may be invisible for a time, but it will be there.

Let me tell you a charming anecdote. During their lifetimes Tolstoy and Turgenev never quite saw eye to eye. Turgenev admired Tolstoy's work, but the admiration was not mutual. Tolstoy thought that the older man was too much devoted to the art of the novel, and too little devoted to life and the purposes to which the novel could be put. There was once a fierce quarrel, and the ominous likelihood of a duel. For years they didn't speak, but in 1878, when he was sixty and Tolstoy was fifty, Turgenev visited the Tolstoy household.

They discussed religion and philosophy, fairly safe subjects since both deal with abstractions. Turgenev played chess with one of the boys, and as a treat read the family one of his tales, which was received politely but without burning enthusiasm. The two novelists then went for a walk through the Tolstoy estate. They came across a seesaw. Looking at the seesaw and then at each other, they were aware of a subtle challenge that each found irresistible. Turgenev got on one end and Tolstoy on the other, and then they were at it, up and down, one moment Turgenev in the ascendant, the next Tolstoy. Of course the Tolstoy children were delighted, as we may be too, not only with the image of the two old boys playing games, but also with the lesson they gave us of the ups and downs of literary principles and literary reputations.

Whom would we put on the seesaw today? Unfortunately— faced with contemporary figures—one's attitude is colored with

irony. The aptest combination I can think of involves a novelist and a critic. In Tolstoy's place, Sir Charles Snow. In Turgenev's, Dr. Leavis. The social purpose novel versus the great
tradition.

Bernard Shaw once said to Joseph Conrad, "Your novels
just won't do, you know." Dickens and Thackeray hated each
other. Wells lampooned Henry James. Attending the funeral of
Sir Hugh Walpole, Somerset Maugham is credited with the remark, "This is the first public function dear Hugh and I have
attended together for years."

Men who have achieved similar measures of recognition and
success in the same field have little to argue about except the
aims and nature of that work. The public will sometimes seem
to settle the argument for them, but the views of one decade
are often reversed by the next. In 1938 Cyril Connolly wrote,
"Strachey, Galsworthy, Bennett, Lawrence, Moore, and Firbank are dead and also out of fashion. They are as if they had
never been. Suppose new manuscripts were discovered, a Five
Towns by Bennett, a Forsyte by Galsworthy, even another novel
by Lawrence. It would be a nightmare." But in 1963, an undis-
covered novel by Lawrence would be greeted by Mr. Connolly
with several column inches in the Sunday *Times*, I don't doubt.
Since 1938 Firbank has had his revival. One feels that Moore
will presently get another inning. A mandarin, searching for
something to exercise his long nails on, will scratch him, and
we shall all itch.

What makes for a revival? If we know, would that help us
to analyze what is abiding in a work of literature? And if we
knew what was abiding, should we be able to assess its value,
and, through that, define what its aims should be?

Unfortunately, we know that a revival is usually arranged
and seldom spontaneous, the result of one or several influential
men drawing our attention to some neglected writer of a previous generation. Such men exist, and we should be thankful

for them, but our inductive method would prove nothing about the aims of literature, it would only tell us something about one man's or several men's personal opinions about those aims, and opinions, naturally enough, differ.

"In my profession as a writer," wrote Goethe, "I have never asked myself how I may be of service to the whole. But always I have only sought to make myself better and more full of insight, to increase the content of my own personality, and then only to express what I had recognised as good and true."

"People don't want works of art from you," our old friend Bernard Shaw said to Henry James. "They want help."

In 1914, James said, "Prose fiction now occupies itself as never before with 'the condition of the people,' a fact quite irrelevant to the nature it has taken on. Works of art are capable of saying more things to man about himself than any other works whatever are capable of doing—and it's only by saying as much to him as possible, by saying, as nearly as we can, all there is, and in as many ways and on as many sides, and with a vividness or presentation that 'art' and 'art alone' is adequate mistress of, that we enable him to pick and choose and compare and know, enable him to arrive at any sort of synthesis that isn't, through all its superficialities and vacancies, a base and illusive humbug."

"We find here," wrote Hazlitt of the novel, "a close imitation of man and manners, we see the very web and texture of society as it really exists, and as we meet it when we come into the world. We are brought acquainted with the motives and characters of mankind, imbibe our notions of virtue and vice from practical examples, and are taught a knowledge of the world through the airy medium of romance."

"For our time," wrote Lionel Trilling, "the most effective agent of the moral imagination has been the novel of the last two hundred years. . . . Its greatness and its practical usefulness is in its unremitting work of involving the reader himself in the moral life, inviting him to put his own motives under examination, suggesting that reality is not as his conventional education has led him to see it. It was the literary form to which the emotions of understanding and forgiveness were indigenous, as if by the definition of the form itself."

"It's no good pretending," Ronald Bryden wrote last year in *The Spectator*, "we can still believe in novels—not as the Victorians took Trollope and George Eliot, seriously as life. We can no longer suspend our disbelief for one man's voice announcing "Here is the world." "Worlds" perhaps—we admit Proust's, Faulkner's, and Anthony Powell's, but those are something smaller and less enfolding. To maintain its weakened hold on some kind of reality, fiction has shrunk from the empire conquered by Dickens, Balzac, and Tolstoy, to the provinces of the short story. When plays stopped pretending to be life, they could begin to be serious statements about reality. Something similar is happening at last in the novel. Novelists are beginning to treat the novel frankly as what it has always been: a toy, a miniature, a puppet-show model."

Does something begin to emerge? Is there, from quotations such as these, a feeling to be had of literature and the novel being lost, like a ball, in the hurly-burly of the scrummage of excuses for it? Is it exactly when the artists and the critics begin to define their art that it is already dying in that definition?

Fifty thousand years ago man penetrated deep into caves and drew pictures of his most powerful enemy, who happened also to be the source of his food and clothing—the aurochs, the bulls. The pictures showed bulls chased, hunted, caught, killed, and disembowelled.

This was man's wish fulfillment, his compensation fantasy, his sympathetic magic. By drawing an image of a mortally wounded bull, he believed this gave him the power to kill it. He didn't know how, he simply believed. He admitted mystery. Artists ever since, although in an increasingly sophisticated way, have been creating images of bulls they think it necessary to slay, the bulls of injustice, intolerance, prejudice, fear, cruelty: bulls that represent all the dangers and evils that threaten man and society. This conscious impulse of the artist seems to me so obvious, even through the layers of sophistication, that I wonder if it is actually possible to conceive of an art, of a literature, that isn't fundamentally a reflection of the human conscience, of the human sense of good and bad. Of course, the primitive sense of good and bad, unlike the primitive senses of smell and hearing, has become more acute. It has expanded more or less simultaneously with the human horizon. Feelings of good and bad changed to concepts of right and wrong when we began to learn that what was good for us might be bad for a lot of other people, and so, in the end, bad for us as well. I should hesitate to claim for the artist too great a credit for helping to refine and extend that sense, although I think that in his age he has always had it in as fine a degree as anyone, and has perhaps pondered over its ramifications more. In fact, it is in his nature to ponder it. Most people are dissatisfied with the world they live in, the artist no less than the social reformer, but whereas the social reformer will take steps to improve the world that actually exists, the artist creates replicas and images and abstractions of that world, and, on the whole, leaves you to draw your own conclusions as to what is wrong with it, by juxtaposing it with the image. He is a cave painter who knows that the magic of his bull images lies demonstrably in the encouragement they give others to kill them, but is that their only value? Should we, sophisticated as we are, altogether exclude the element of mystery—the mystery of the image itself, which, created as it may have been for a recognizable purpose, now exists in its own right? Who cares *why* the Mona Lisa smiles? But how grateful we are that she does.

Perhaps it isn't surprising that in Spain, where they still kill bulls, they also believe in what they call the *duende*. It means imp, or ghost, or goblin. It is the force in an artist that he cannot explain, the force, you may call it, of his sympathetic magic. Lorca said that the duende burned the blood like powdered glass. Another Spaniard, Manuel Torres, said that everything that had dark sounds had the duende.

I think this is true. The duende is inside, so the sounds that come are bound to be dark. I think of the novelist's duende as a little black hunchback chained to the wall of his dungeon, whose job it is to draw pictures on the walls, pictures that have to be interpreted in words. When you find his pictures moving, he may shriek with laughter. When you find them comic, you may hear him weeping in the straw. He is both tempter and conscience, a concert in himself of good and evil. He is his own creator and his own critic. When I read other people's novels I look for signs that the duende has been at work. When Jim Dixon burned holes in the blankets in *Lucky Jim*, the duende was overcome with shame and remorse while laughing himself sick. He swung on the chandelier with the girl in Iris Murdoch's *Flight from the Enchanter*, and waved a samurai sword in *A Severed Head*. He lost the feeling in his fingers and toes when he watched the burnt-out case stump about the leprosy in Mr. Greene's novel of that name. Through the whole of Nabokov's *Pale Fire* he saw wild ivy growing on the pavements of an American university town. He felt his own forehead for the bumps of incipient horns when he met Dougal Douglas in *The Ballad of Peckham Rye*, and hid in a corner of the taxi with Joe

Lampton when they said at the end of *Room at the Top* that Joe wasn't to blame for Alice's death, and Joe said, "Oh my God, that's the trouble." He felt the horror and excitement of release from moral obligations when Golding's children painted their faces in *Lord of the Flies*. And he was there on the cliff top, alternately capering and catching when Salinger wrote that memorable passage, which is just about as socially conscious as you can get without being too obvious:

> I'm standing on the edge of some crazy cliff. What I have to do, I have to catch everybody if they start to go over the cliff—I mean if they're running and they don't look where they're going. I have to come out from somewhere and catch them. That's all I'd do all day. I'd just be the catcher in the rye and all. I know it's crazy, but that's the only thing I'd like to be.

This is the subjective way of looking at novels, and where there is a subjective way there must be an objective way as well. If we admit that a novel exists in its own right, we're then entitled to ask: What is it? Why is it? even if the answers aren't especially informative. Those are critical questions, in the sense that critics ask them. What I'm trying to do here is draw a distinction betwen the critical attitude that says: Here is a work of literature: What is it? Why is it? and the other and more general attitude that says: The novel is a serious statement about reality; or: The novel is a prose work of ideas and images which must be serviceable to mankind, accessible and comprehensible to everyone; or: The novel is an agent of the moral imagination; therefore, to what extent does this particular work accord with this principle or these principles? In other words: To what extent is this work novel?

It seems to me that one of the dangers of this kind of critical definition, and perhaps one of the dangers teachers of literature have to face, is to make the writing of novels seem all too easy. Any reasonably intelligent boy or girl who has learned to read and to write and to make some kind of moral judgment of the world about him may have only to be told that a novel is, say, an imitation of man and manners to think himself capable of writing one. A worse danger, in this literate but undiscriminating age, is that it will probably be published, and he will write *more*. Writing a novel has become an incidental proof of social and intellectual status. It's become what you do if you can't think of anything better. Asked by a publisher to remove the four-letter words from his manuscript, a young first novelist said: "But I couldn't. I could never face my friends if I published a novel without at least *one*." Such a boy or girl may well feel strongly about the state of modern society. But shouldn't he be encouraged more to become a journalist, or a welfare worker, or to go into local politics? Especially today, when the expanding means of disseminating information and opinion have released the novel from one of its old incidental roles? Don't go on the stage, people have always said, and still say; Don't, for heaven's sake, expect to get anywhere writing poetry; Why on earth do you want to paint? But—Have you heard? Our John is writing his first novel.

The two books Mr. Bryden was reviewing in his article in *The Spectator*, which went under the title *Living Dolls*, were *Franny and Zooey* and *An Unofficial Rose*. He said:

"No longer required to persuade you of what he narrates, only of what he means by it, the novelist can invent, fantasticate, button-hole, and pattern as he pleases. You re-admit, as it were, the miraculous, the pleasure of pure formality—and in the old sense—style."

I hadn't been aware that invention, fantastication, the miraculous, formality, and style had yet been denied to writers ever, and certainly not in this century, which is the century of Kafka, Woolf, Joyce, Huxley, Hemingway, Greene, Faulkner, and Nabokov, and of George Orwell, whose pigs learned to walk on their hind legs. I had not been aware of these exclusions either in whole or in part, but I hope that Mr. Bryden in future reviews will not submit every novel he comes across to the tests he has not so much supplied to as deduced from these two modern works. Are they in fact to be applied now to *War and Peace*, *Bleak House*, and *Washington Square* to prove somehow that those three novels are no longer valid as novels, or are we to understand that once a novel has been one thing it can never be that thing again, or only that thing again after a decent interval?

What have we so far seemed to show? That literature—the novel—defies definition? Or that in the wake of the novelists, an intelligent job has nearly always been done of answering the questions, What is it? Why is it? But that the tendency has been to turn a particular answer into a general theory of the novel, and that the theory, once expounded, has about as much to do with living literature as a postmortem has to do with a living body?

When Mr. Nabokov refused an invitation last year to attend a writer's conference in Edinburgh, he was told, "But Mr. Nabokov, we're to discuss the problems and the future of the novel." To which he splendidly replied, "I'm only interested in the problems and future of my own."

Because you are teachers, perhaps I have labored this point unnecessarily. Teachers are not critics. Teachers are concerned to deal with the whole body of literature as though it were alive in all its limbs, and not moribund in all but a few questing fingers and toes. You may therefore agree with me that this whole body of literature—from earliest beginnings to modern times—has fundamentally always been a literature of *dissent*, if only because no man will bother to create anything if he thinks a good job has been done already by God and man.

Poor Cinderella. Is it fair that she should scour the pots and pans while her sisters, all the big wide world, go to the ball? Poor Desdemona. Poor Jane Eyre. Poor Oliver Twist. Poor Uncle Tom. Even, poor Becky Sharp. The lessons of injustice and inhumanity are learned very early, and we respond to them, even as children who are surrounded by love and happiness and comfort. It is as though we are born with a racial memory of pain and misfortune.

So is Trilling right when he says that the most effective agent of the moral imagination has been the novel of the last two hundred years? I think he may be. He was echoing Hazlitt's remark about imbibing notions of virtue and vice through the airy medium of romance, and of course referring back to Shelley's unacknowledged legislators. But is there a danger lurking here for the author? Should he see lessons in morality as an effect, a by-product of literature, or as its cause, its excuse for existence? Let's go back to Mr. Connolly, whose book was written towards the end of an era especially notable for the political commitment of its leading writers, the era that ended with the close of the Civil War in Spain and the opening of the shooting war in Europe. He said:

> Writers flourish in a state of political flux, on the eve of the crisis, rather than in the crisis itself. . . . It is before a war or a revolution that they are listened to. They are politically minded when they are able to accomplish something . . . on the eve before the resort to arms takes matters out of their control.
>
> But there are dangers about being political of which writers are unaware and so seldom avoid. Being political is apt to become a whole-time job . . . and the activity leads to disillusion. And if we look back at the political activities of artists, however necessary or satisfying they have seemed at the time, now that time is past it is not by them they are remembered.

This rings fairly true. And there is another point. If there is anything worse for a writer than missing the bus, it is being thought, twenty years later, to have got on the wrong one. Is there another point still? Behind the social, human activity of politics there are theories of morality, but they are theories that call for strong physical and emotional involvement to be put into practice. Does the disillusionment of the politically committed writer spring also from the sense he may have of being involved in rabble-rousing?

Let's consider a particular word: statement. It's a critic's word, an attempt to pin down a work of art to the level of the targets it hits, to the questions it answers. This is quite fair; after all, it's one of the critic's tasks. But should the author commit himself, like a public figure, to the questions he thinks he has an answer to, or to those that will, in the end, remain formidable mysteries to him? If he too consciously commits himself to answering what he thinks are answerable questions, will he become a writer of instructive literature, and will that make him, if he isn't careful, a journalist, a pamphleteer, perhaps a legislator-manqué? Is a novel that is a work of art embarked upon by its author in a frame of mind that admits certainty or preconceived opinions? The images he builds up will contain statements about life and society, good and evil, but should they be the images of a dissenting, inquiring mind, or of a dissenting, instructing one? Writing a novel is like peeling an onion. Even Tolstoy, who said literature was rubbish, wept over his manuscripts. But that is not what I mean. I mean that if you peel away the skins of pros and cons, should you find yourself with a kernel of truth, or with the seed of another onion?

Critics tend only to see the skins. They look at the pulpy mess and ask: What does it say? What does it mean? What is its statement? If the aim of literature is to say something, to mean something, to make a statement in terms other than itself, does it follow that the statements it makes must be statements of major contemporary significance, if it is to be major literature? If so, what major statements should a writer be making today? Should we all be making the same one? And are we committed by our statements to actions in support of them?

What, in Sartre's definition, is *our* unique historical situation?

Today we don't have Hitler, that rotten but dangerous log thrown into and damming the riverbed of what I call the moral drift of history. Instead we have an antagonist, to whom there is no appeal because the antagonist is beyond reason, beyond feeling. The enemy today is symptomatic of today, being unhuman, faceless, mindless, and yet still, curiously, a character. We can't effectively march against this character with lyrics and bullets, apply sanctions, or get up a subscription or parcel of warm clothing for its victims. It exists, terribly, the irrevocable monster of our inventive civilization. The bomb. The unpredictable commandant of a vast concentration camp in which we all have numbers tatooed on our arms, and all wear stars of Jerusalem on our paper shirts, and all wonder how long it will be before we are made into soap for a world that no longer needs to wash or into lampshades for a people who have gone beyond the need to distinguish between dark and light.

Men and women of my own and later generations may be forgiven if we find it difficult to draw a moral distinction between a bomb, however big, and a bullet, however small; if we fail to turn up at Aldermaston, or to interfere with simple Yankee sailors in the execution of their duty at Holy Loch; forgiven too if we rather fail in enthusiastic response to what has been called the new wave of satire which, in the event, turns out to be directed at all those old Aunt Sallies of church, throne, and state, and in its quality to fall rather short of the satirical standards of the seventeenth and eighteenth centuries. Above all, perhaps we can be forgiven if we feel that liberal views can be expressed only by liberal voices, and liberal values fought for only with liberal weapons, and forgiven finally if we don't quite see how this can effectively be done. We don't have Nanking and Dachau, we have the Congo and Cape Town. But we had our shooting war against tyranny, and its end-product was the Bomb. All that really happened when we fought fascism was that our bullets grew bigger. When young people say Ban the

Bomb, their moral justification is that they mean ban the bullet and all weapons of destructive force. But do they decry a show of force from Washington to ensure the safety of Negro students in Southern universities?

But perhaps Sartre meant us to take a more insular view. In a recent and notably well-argued book, *A State of England,* the author, Mr. Anthony Hartley, assistant editor of *The Spectator,* wrote:

> The general thesis I wish to put forward is that the diminution of Great Britain's position in the world and the relatively narrow economic margin on which we have lived since the war have caused a narrowing of horizons and a sense of frustration in English society, which has frequently, though not always consciously, been expressed by English intellectuals. And this claustrophobia has been made worse by disappointment at the result of the advent of the welfare state. Thus, the culminating success and slow decline of the two great movements of reform—the establishment of the welfare state society at home and the liquidation of the British colonial empire abroad—have not only left us with a shortage of ideals but also with the residual bitterness of seeing them turn out rather differently from what we expected.

Although young people may feel that, like greatness, the liquidation of the British colonial empire was a moral reform thrust upon us from outside and that the welfare state was really a Tory plot to make every worker a property owner in his own right, Mr. Hartley's thesis is a cogent summary of the English liberal dilemma of the 1960s. The world we have is the world we and our predecessors fought for with every kind of weapon and moral equipment. Now, as men and women in society, we have a feeling that even if we knew what action should be taken to further the pursuit of human happiness, the results of that action would prove no more effective than those we have taken in the past. I feel discomfort; therefore, I am alive. The quotation comes from Graham Greene's *A Burnt-out Case,* as does the following:

> A vocation is an act of love; it is not a professional career. When desire is dead one cannot continue to make love. I've come to the end of desire and to the end of a vocation. Don't try to blind me in a loveless marriage, and to make me imitate what I used to perform with passion. And don't talk to me like a priest about my duty. A talent . . . should not be buried when it still has purchasing power, but when the currency has changed—and no value is left in the coin. Obsolete coins, like corn, have always been found in graves.

A somewhat similar image emerges early on in Iris Murdoch's novel, *An Unofficial Rose:*

> Can't you see me fading away before your eyes, can't everyone see it? I need a different world, a formal world; I need form, structure, will, something to encounter, something to make me *be.* Form, as this rose has it. That's what Ann hasn't got. She's as messy and flabby as a bloody dogrose. That's what gets me down. That's what destroys all my imagination, all the bloody footholds.

In such distinguished company I'm not sure that I should quote from my own work, but the following passage in a novel published at approximately the same time as these other two does, perhaps, further illuminate the same dilemma of desire and personality in relation to action and will:

> There wasn't a square inch of earth that hadn't been discovered, trampled on, littered with cigarette ends and

Kwikkaffy tins; not a square mile of ocean that hadn't seen the passage of a million balsa-wood rafts; not a social or political concept that hadn't been tried, tested and discredited, not an idea that hadn't been had before and been applied and then disowned; not an instinct that hadn't been written up by Freud or Jung, not a microbe that hadn't been bottled by Pasteur or Fleming, nor an act of mercy left unperpetrated by UNNRA or Schweitzer. It had all been done. The moulds were cast. They only had to be serviced, filled with the molten sub-standard iron of inherited good intentions and up-ended to produce little tombstones of inferior, repeat performances.

Readers may feel that these are passages from what is sometimes called the literature of despair. But they ask more about the uncertain future than they tell about the unsatisfactory present. Implicitly they assume a future and ask what action can be taken that will be, now, for human good. Even more obviously socially conscious novels like *Lucky Jim* and *Room at the Top* seem to me to ask this question. Behind the bare narration of events—and the events in both books show young men making their way in a society that attracts them and yet repels them—behind the narration that seems so often simply to be telling us: This is how it is, isn't there the question: *How better might it be?*

I spoke a while ago of what I call the moral drift of history. I use the word drift to conjure the image of movement—slow, sluggish, but still movement—and couple it with the word moral to show that the movement I have in mind is a movement in what I hope is a desirable direction. This is the kind of river that will never, within our comprehension, reach the sea, but in spite of that we clear the riverbed, bit by bit, to let the water through. I also spoke a moment ago of the rotten but dangerous logs that sometimes fall into the riverbed, struck by the lightning of their own passions. Because we are engaged, as men and women in society, whether we are artists, artisans, administrators, or laborers, because we're engaged in a job of engineering, we have to cope with the detail while keeping our eye on the pattern as a whole. In the thirties the detail that took our attention was the rotten log of fascism and anti-semitism, aspects of our basic enemy: injustice. On other historical occasions, it has been the rotten log of religious bigotry, industrial slavery, colonial exploitation, or—to go further back—brute and superstitious ignorance.

If as artists, we are to prove our social conscience, if we are to show that our social conscience is the sine qua non of our artistic endeavor, then surely we are committed to the detail as well as to the completion of the overall plan? If so, then we are clearly obligated to get rid of the log that is damming the stream up at the moment. What is the main one? My own belief is that the log at present damming the stream up is that of racial prejudice. But does this make Mr. James Baldwin the most significant modern novelist? Will his art live longer than that of Mr. L. P. Hartley or Mr. James Hanley? And if I feel so strongly about this as a member of society, as I do, should I commit myself to the writing of novels that will expose the evil from every possible angle? Should I shrug off as relatively unimportant the sudden urge I might have to write a novel about a love affair between a white man and a white woman on an uninhabited island?

Or, if we are to forget racial prejudice, and take it that the obstructing log is that of the welfare state gone bad, does that make *Lucky Jim* and *Room at the Top* better novels than *Pale Fire* and *A Burnt-out Case*? Or, is Mr. Hartley's theory of the claustrophobia that is frequently but not always consciously expressed by English intellectuals at once an explanation of the artificially closed circle of Miss Murdoch's novels and proof that Miss Murdoch has more to say, to us, and to future generations, than Mrs. Muriel Spark, who more patently admits, because of her religious convictions, of a power outside that circle, a power that sets it in motion and disrupts it as surely as that little devilkin Dougal Douglas disrupted the modern affluent society of Peckham Rye? Is the sophisticated despair of A *Catcher in the Rye* more contemporaneously significant than the allegorical despair of *Lord of the Flies*? Are each of these writers moved by social conscience? Are some more moved than others? Are those who seem to be more moved actually more moved? If so, is their work of greater value? Or is it simply that, being writers of their time, they cannot help but reflect the moods of their time, and whatever else they bring to their work that is timeless is what matters? Is it that the historical interest of a novel is the first thing that dies in a novel, and is it the contemporary significance of today that becomes the historical interest of tomorrow?

I spoke a while ago of the waxing and waning moon of literary principles and literary reputations. May I complete the metaphor by reminding us that the moon I speak of has a dark side to it? It is the dark side of a novel that I wait to sense the existence of, and to the dark sounds that I try to listen. What lies behind *Pale Fire*? Of all the recent novels I have read, this is the one that most fully engaged me. It is, of course, in Mr. Bryden's terms, a distinguished literary conceit, a game, a toy, a puppet-show—and you might say the same of Stendhal's *Charterhouse of Parma*, as well as *An Unofficial Rose*. But whereas it is possible to hazard a guess and say that Stendhal was asking: What is justice? What is desire? What is love? and arriving at no conclusion, and whereas it is also possible to guess that Miss Murdoch is asking: What is reality? What is will?—asking but not answering, because the asking is enough—I find it virtually impossible to suggest what Mr. Nabokov is asking in *Pale Fire*. And this is what interests me, because in spite of that, the whole book seems to vibrate with questions and, in doing so, to convey an impression of life as a continuity instead of as a series of objectives that become dead ends.

188

"I shall continue to exist," his narrator says in the last page. "I may assume other disguises, other forms, but I shall try to exist. I may turn up yet, on another campus, as an old, happy, healthy, heterosexual Russian, a writer in exile, sans fame, sans future, sans audience, sans everything but his art."

I have tried through quotations and commentary to define, as clearly as I can, my own way of looking at a novel. Can it make any appeal to you as teachers? Is it possible to lead those whom you teach through the dense jungle of ephemeral opinions, statements, beliefs, and judgments, towards—again to quote James—any sort of synthesis that isn't, through all its superficialities and vacancies, a base and illusive humbug? Is it possible to discuss a work of literature on the basis that when all that is known about it has been considered, when it has been analyzed in terms of its historical context, proven or disproven in terms of its social significance, regarded in terms of its texture, color, rhythm, and form, it is the residual element of mystery that is important, the curious paradox of the illusion of a better life existing in an artifice that still truthfully reflects the ills of the life we know?

Who will bother to create such an artifice who is satisfied with what already exists? All art is the product of dissatisfaction. Is it true to say that the greater the dissatisfaction the greater the artist? If so, how do we measure dissatisfaction? By its intensity or by its scope? If an artist directs and concentrates his dissatisfaction, will his effects be greater? Is it a good thing that they should be? Or is he then using the novel to criticize an aspect of society that he feels strongly critical of as a man, at the expense of other aspects, establishing himself in society as a spokesman of a cause, and thereby making himself that much less an artist? Should the artist in him also be critical of the cause he is committed to as a man? Is the cause inimical to the artist? Or does he do his finest work once he has actively embraced it? These are problems novelists and poets especially have always pondered, because their medium is the word and the word is an instrument of direct communication. Should they use words to create something so that it may exist in its own right, or to create something that may exist in order to demolish what exists and is undesirable?

Our powers are limited. It is tempting to concentrate them, to tell ourselves: This I know, therefore this I can say. The alternative is the loneliness of the desk and the questions: What do I know? What can I say? If I write it, shall I know what I know, and know what I've said, or simply expose greater depths of my desire for human happiness?

It is also tempting to run away from the bleak landscape of technical uncertainty and technical dissatisfaction and say: That kind of novel is dead, this is what it should be. Tempting to belong to a school, tempting to laugh and plan and drink mugs of hot cocoa in cold committee rooms, to be needed, to be questioned, to tell, to be listened to, to be loved, and to be criticized and hated and burned in effigy and shown every sign that you too actually exist and are a useful, even an essential member of the society you would like to change.

Can we reach a synthesis that Henry James would accept? Art, Tolstoy said, is a human activity. Therefore, to write a novel that is a work of art is to take an action. The sum of such actions in the past two hundred years, according to Trilling, has been the most effective agent of man's moral imagination, especially, to paraphrase Connolly, during periods of political flux, when men and women are most conscious of discomfort, and therefore of wanting what Shaw would call help, even though history and experience have taught them that in the wake of actions they take to help themselves and others, there usually follows a period of disillusion. But in that period of disillusion, the artist will again stand up and point the way to the next stage of the journey to the promised land. This perhaps explains *Resurrection*, but does it explain *Washington Square*? or Ford Madox Ford's beautiful novel, *The Good Soldier*?

Is the one valid explanation of art, and therefore of the novel, that it is an action taken by a man or a woman in an attempt to reach beyond his own disillusion, beyond the proven futility of action in the world of reality? Shouldn't he distrust the limitations imposed on a man in the world of real action, and accept only the limitations, commit himself only to the limitations of action in his chosen field? And isn't it because he never really knows those limitations that he continues to act, as an artist, with an almost inhuman optimism, without disillusion, without a sense of futility, no matter how bitter his personal disappointments as an artist and as a man? And isn't it this example, this sense of there being somewhere a life without disillusion, a life without futility, that—communicated to other people—justifies the artist as a man going about his mysterious business in the world of ordinary affairs? Isn't it when he feels that art is not enough—that he must justify it in terms of something other than itself—that he abdicates his uncomfortable vocation, and, lining himself up as a more obvious contributor to society, is then subject to the laws and prejudices of that society, and in the long run sinks with it into the quicksands of its own disillusion?

"A life's work," so Faulkner described his novels, "a life's work in the agony and sweat of the human spirit, not for glory, and least of all for profit, but to create out of the materials of the human spirit something which did not exist before." To the extent that he succeeded, then, to what immediate *use*, other than its own, can something that didn't exist before be put by a society that has no standards to judge it by? To the extent that he didn't succeed, to the extent that no author succeeds in his aim, should he ever lose sight of it? Should he consciously bend his acts to the uses of public action? Or should he be content with the action of art, which may be the only kind of human action that doesn't directly challenge the *humanity* of those who hold contrary opinions to his own? The only kind of action that *refreshes,* like a cloth dipped in wine, instead of in vinegar?

A WRITER
TAKES STOCK

◆

[At the time Scott wrote to Mollie Hamilton that he was feeling deskbound and was working intensely on A Division of the Spoils, he nevertheless accepted an invitation to become president of the London Writers Circle. "A Writer Takes Stock" was delivered to the members of that group on October 22, 1973, in what amounted to a presidential address. This text is immensely valuable, because it presents what Scott called an "autobiography of the writer in me." He gives information about himself, as both an incipient and a mature writer, that is nowhere else available, information that suggests that he began to develop the ability to conceive dialogue, scene, and structure as a child filmmaker. He also tells here how his wife supported him as a writer and became a writer herself.]

One of the first things I did after accepting the very kind, and very flattering, invitation to become president of this circle, was to look up in a dictionary the meaning of the intransitive verb *preside*. According to *Chambers Dictionary*, it means to be in the chair, to superintend, and, which may surprise you—it certainly surprised me—to be at the organ or the piano as a kind of conductor.

The first two of these functions already being more than adequately taken care of by your chairman and your committee, and unable actually to play a note, I am somewhat at a loss to know *how* to perform, as president. And so—in order not to remain for too long, simply as a name on the letterheads—it seemed to me a good idea to make my opening talk a brief essay in autobiography.

One advantage the autobiographer has over the novelist is that he knows where to begin. For instance, I was born in 1920. With that statement the advantage ends, because this is the autobiography of *the writer* in me. When was *he* born? When, to borrow a term from the physicists, did he go critical?

I think at the age of six. It was certainly at the age of six that I made my first mark on the literary world, not merely by reading *Three Weeks* by Elinor Glyn, but by taking one of my father's 3B pencils and defacing the title page of every one of the volumes in his edition of the Waverley novels. I did this because I had confused Sir Walter Scott with an uncle whom I detested. I had just got to the last volume, volume two of Lockhart's biography, when my mother came into the room, saw what I had done and said: "Wait. Wait Until Your Father Sees This."

Well, Father saw it. Fortunately it turned out that he was himself a Dickens and Thackeray man, and was mainly concerned at the waste of his 3B pencil, which (he gently pointed out), although encased in wood, did not grow on trees.

My father was a commercial artist. He did fashion plates and specialized in furs. Because the autumn catalogues were always published in August or September, the wholesale and retail furriers used to send their stuff to him in the spring and early summer. Cascades of mink, and astrakhan, silver fox, musquash, and the despised rabbit tumbled out of the immense brown paper parcels which came by Carter Paterson and the LNER [London and North Eastern Railway]—and covered his summer studio ankle deep in winter opulence. My mother, who sometimes posed for him, one hand on hip, the other indicating a vista, always complained that the only time she wore sable was in June, when it was too hot to enjoy it.

Although self-employed, my father didn't work at home. He had two homes. Or rather one and a half. He rented the houses which from time to time my mother, my brother, and I lived in—and he slept in—and paid half the rent of another house where he had his studio and which was lived in by his two spinster sisters. The elder of these was his partner, my Aunt Florrie. She did faces, hands, legs, and feet, and sometimes toned down the shadows of his overexuberant bosoms. Art steps in where nature fails. He set off every morning about nine o'clock and sometimes didn't come home until nine o'clock at night. The two houses were about a mile apart. All this was in North London, in what was known as the urban district of Southgate, at that time on the borders of Hertfordshire.

Perhaps it was the early lesson about the flatness of life and the rotundity of art that lies at the bottom of my attitude to things around me.

In that same summer of 1926, when I was six, I became a picturegoer. The first film I saw—silent, of course—was called *The Keeper of the Bees*. I remember absolutely nothing about *The Keeper of the Bees*, but know that from that moment on, for at least a decade, I was a dedicated, fanatical film fan. And within three years, that's to say by 1929, my brother and I had set up in the film business as producers, directors, designers, and photographers.

My father and my Aunt Florrie were not the only artists in the Scott family and its closely related family of Scott-Wright cousins. We are supposed to have descended through a niece from the naturalist and engraver, Thomas Bewick, and both my brother and I inherited some facility with pencils, brushes, and pen and ink.

The films we produced were drawn in India ink, with mapping pens, on long narrow strips of greaseproof or tracing paper, which were gummed together and passed through a projector made out of a cigar box, a sixty-watt bulb, and the lens from an old pair of binoculars. The images we drew were freehand. Frames of dialogue were interspersed to help the stories along.

When it came to close-ups of the leading characters, we traced these from photographs of popular stars. The whole was projected on to a screen painted silver and authentically edged in black.

The business of making films absorbed me for about four years. When my elder brother grew out of this exacting occupation, he contributed technical assistance. The projector became infinitely more sophisticated. The screen was only revealed to the audience after a velvet curtain had been raised by invisible wires and had disappeared mysteriously behind an immense gilded proscenium arch made of painted plywood. By this time, too, my films were running for sixty minutes and had also become more sophisticated, with some sequences in color. Romance, drama, comedy, costume, and modern—one film would take me an entire autumn to complete, to be ready for its Christmas gala release. I suppose we never gave more than two shows a year. The *creation* of the film was the main thing. The stories were all more or less original, but the stars were real, subcontracted from Paramount, Fox, R.K.O., and Metro-Goldwyn-Mayer. My last epic was a sophisticated comedy called *The Girl in the Porch,* and starred Miriam Hopkins, Alice White (making a comeback) and Fredric March. Coming across it years later and riffling it through my fingers, I noted that scenically it was distinctly avant-garde. And script-wise, just a little naughty. Unconsciously so, I think. But at last I understood a remark by my headmaster that while this boy's English essays showed promise, he lacked discrimination.

The business of creating a plot and characters seemed to come perfectly naturally. Unconsciously I had absorbed the lessons of the cinema and also of the many books I had now read. By the time I was fourteen I was growing out of the cinema business and becoming more aware of the power of words without pictures. Required to write compositions of not less than three pages, I found difficulty in covering less than twelve—and once produced eighteen, about a traveler lost on the moors.

I had been no further afield than Worthing and Eastbourne, so was hardly a seasoned traveler, and I had never seen a moor in my life, but I remember overhearing my English master say to another master, after this composition had been handed around, "Scott 2"—my brother was known as Scott 1—"Scott 2," he said, "could be an author if he wanted to be."

Being a perverse boy, I decided then and there to be an artist instead, or perhaps a film director. Or even actor. Writing was obviously too easy. It was with some surprise that eventually I heard that my father had decided that I should become an accountant.

I never did become an accountant in the qualified sense. But it was a near thing. Or was it? For a year or so before the war, working during the day in an office in Regent Street, or sallying forth for a day's auditing in Streatham, with my sandwiches in my briefcase, and in the evenings immersed in the mysteries of double-entry, depreciation, and wear and tear, I never once, never once convinced myself of my impersonation. I did not feel like an accountant. I did not feel like an accountant because although my mind was on it, my heart wasn't in it. I was now quite clear in my mind that I felt like a writer, and sometimes, pushing aside my textbook on mercantile law, I would borrow an hour or two to jot down a work of whose genius I had no doubt: a story, a poem, once a three-act play. The play was about a family very different from my own and was set—as I'm sure you've guessed—in their drawing-room, which was considerably more luxurious than any I had ever entered.

And, playing truant from the law of diminishing returns (to which perhaps, as an author, I might have paid *more* attention), I was discovering Auden, Eliot, Isherwood, Ibsen, Chekhov—a whole pantheon of modern literary gods—and renewing acquaintance with some of the older, including Walter Scott, who had his revenge one day when I looked up from the pages of *The Antiquary* and found that the tube had long since gone past Holborn, where I should have changed, and had arrived at a curious place called South Kensington.

I saw myself as a poet and playwright. As yet the world of the novel seemed too vast and laborious. Aged eighteen, I had begun one. It was called *Rachel* and was set in Bloomsbury. The only contacts I'd had with Bloomsbury were the second-hand bookshops within a stone's throw of the office of a Spanish importer of Canary Island tomatoes, whose books I tried to keep in order. I never discovered who Rachel was because my hero, arriving from the North, where I had also never been, reached Kings Cross with his suitcases, walked to Fitzroy Square, and then ran out of inspiration. So, of course, did I.

But in between casting up the trial balances, I had had time to write about ten poems. And I was so convinced of their merit that—having seen an advertisement, perhaps in the *New Statesman,* which I took religiously because I had become a radical and a follower of Professor Joad—I sent them to a firm called The Cambridge Literary Agency.

It didn't surprise me at all when I had back a letter undertaking to offer three of them to suitable editors. All I had to do was send them two shillings and sixpence for each poem to cover the cost of postage to and fro. Being skint as usual, I borrowed the seven shillings and sixpence from my mother, who insisted for several days thereafter on referring to me as the "future poet laureate." This did not actually irritate me. I merely felt that she was a little premature.

I now underwent my apprenticeship in the first of the writer's disciplines: watching every morning for the postman. Day after day, week after week. But with each passing day my self-confidence grew. The reason for the delay was obvious. The editors whom the agency had approached were obtaining the opinions of men like Eliot, Spender, and C. Day Lewis, who were probably all in Capri or Corfu, but would hasten back soon enough when they had read my stuff.

While waiting for Eliot, Spender, and Lewis, I wasn't idle. Instinctively, I knew a writer never should be. I was preparing new poems to ensure that I had a major body of mature work to show them when they got round to sending for me. Between poems I dashed off the occasional one-act play, to keep my hand in, and three short stories which the *Evening News* was bound to take.

My only real problem was that all this stuff was in hand-written manuscript. I had bashed out the poems now being handled by the agency on the office typewriter while its owner was at lunch. I still use the same two fingers. But a short story and a play were another matter. Use of a typewriter would have to wait until Auden, Eliot, and Isherwood had grabbed me for the Faber list and insisted on lending me one of their own machines so that I could prepare the typescript of a first collection. This would be published in boards. I would have a pale-green cloth, quarter bound in slightly darker-green leather. I designed the colophon in the form of a tasteful sprig of lime blossom, whose smell then reminded me of nothing so much as the hopes and ambitions of youth, but which I have since learned to connect with the smells of funerals.

And then, one day, there was an envelope bearing the printed name of the Cambridge Literary Agency. Too thick for just a letter. Proofs perhaps?

No. Not proofs. The poems. My first professional failure. I returned the seven shillings and sixpence to my mother and told her I would have to change my agent. I didn't tell her that the poems had been sent only to magazines with names like *Great Thoughts* and *The Lady*.

After this failure, however, came my first *success*.

Now I know that in this circle you keep a "success book," and that right at the bottom of the categories in which success may be claimed come *letters*. And I suspect that success in this category is considered very modest indeed. *What I have to tell*

*you as your new president is that my own first published work was
a letter. Not only my first, but my second. And my third. And my
fourth.* For each of the first two I earned half a crown. The third
and fourth earned nothing because they were letters to the local
paper. The two which were paid for were letters of film criticism to *The Picturegoer.*

And I know that this *is* success, because it is proof that one
can put words together and convey an idea. And the name,
Paul Scott, in print, seemed to give me an identity which I had
been groping for. It was a name which I felt everyone was surely
going to hear a great deal more of.

They didn't, of course. Not there. Not in that house where
we now lived. Although it was in that house that all this rather
comic but I think rather touching energy and enthusiasm and
self-confidence began to be put together and disciplined. In that
new house, I was lucky.

And how lucky I had been already. No one had ever dis-
couraged me. No one had ever laughed at me, at least not to
my face. But that of course isn't quite enough. I was lucky mainly
because, not only was I never *dis*couraged, I was—at this early
stage—actively *en*couraged.

This was June 1939. The house next door to the one we
had just moved into was let into two flats. I arrived home one
evening and my mother said she had met our upstairs neighbor.
Knowing that my mother never took long to know who people
were and what they did I said, "Tell me about them." She
didn't know the wife, but the husband was a professor of pho-
netics and a poet. I asked his name. She told me. I said I had
never heard of him. She said "That's what he said about you
when I said you were a poet too, so I gave him some of your
things to prove it."

Well, *he was* a poet, a poet and a man of letters. There
were proofs of another kind in his flat, galley proofs—and letters from publishers, a postcard from Bernard Shaw, a letter

from Richard Church. His wife was a teacher but also wrote.

Books had always played a part in my family's life, but they were not literary people. I don't think that was a disadvantage, but any member of this circle whose only contact with other writers has been, or is, through membership here, will, I think, know what I mean when I say how lucky I was to have, so early on, two older people who were part of the world I wanted to enter and who were willing to help and encourage me.

But, as I said, it was June 1939. There were really only a few months to benefit from their friendship and kindly advice. Only a few months, but I was in prolific vein. On September 3, I put away the Laws Relating to Bankruptcy and Receiverships—my parents quite understood—so that I could spend my last few months of freedom letting loose the three muses of poetry, prose, and drama.

Under the encouragement I got from next door, I began imperceptibly to suppress impulses which produced the kind of work which they tenderly put to death with a few well-chosen but not hurtful words, and—greedy for praise—give fuller rein to impulses which produced work they took more seriously, because in it they heard—not echoes, but the faint sound of my own voice.

Even now, after all these years, I couldn't say in what way my writer's voice differs from anyone else's. But I know when I have written anything that muffles or falsifies it.

During those few months of freedom I must have written many things. All I remember now are a play and a sequence of poems, both of which were my response to the war. The play, although allegorical, was much more me than the poem, which was in the style of Eliot, but nothing ever came of it. It was about people rebuilding things after a disaster, in a spirit of optimism. A city, no less. It sounds and was frightful. After the war a little theater talked about producing it behind gauze, which would no doubt have been some alleviation of the audience's distress. Fortunately they were spared it altogether.

The sequence of poems had a different fate. It was published. But apart from having written it, and typed it on my neighbor's typewriter, that was none of my doing. For I had departed one bright morning, with my hair already cut shorter than seemed likely, and wended my way to report to the army in Slough, intoning those memorial lines of the man who has recently become poet laureate in my stead [John Betjeman]:

> Come, Friendly Bombs and Fall on Slough
> It isn't fit for humans, now.

Actually Slough wasn't all that bad, and the bombs didn't fall on it while I was there. What fell was the regimental barber's scissor on my already shorn head, as if to prove that while I felt no more like a soldier than I had felt like an accountant, a soldier I now undoubtedly was, at least nominally.

And nominally I remained one for six years, half of them abroad in India and the Far East. But during those six years several apparently important things happened. Through my neighbor's efforts, the poem sequence was published in a series of wartime broadsheets brought out by a young officer, and I had a poem—the only one I wrote in the army—accepted by *Poetry Quarterly*. Neither publication was paid for, and the first thing I knew in both cases was the arrival of proofs, which I didn't know how to correct.

This was in 1940–41. In an especially odd way I felt detached from both events. There is nothing so uncompromising as cold print. Looking at my poems thus, I discerned that perhaps I wasn't a poet after all. This didn't bother me a great deal, because by now I knew that I was a dramatist. Severely curtailed as my opportunities to write were, I did seize every one that was available. In 1942, in Devonshire, I wrote a three-act play about the fate of a community of Jews in an unidentified European country. For reasons that I'll explain, I was able to type this and send a copy to my ex-neighbor. Three years later, while I was in Malaya, I heard that he had submitted it to an international competition for plays on a Jewish theme, and that it had come among the four chosen for publication by Victor Gollancz. Performance was not promised but sounded likely. You will understand how I returned home in 1946 all too well prepared to respond gracefully to the enthusiastic cries of "Author!" I was now twenty-six, and it seemed to be about time. I was as full as ever of creative energy and enthusiasm and self-confidence. I had two more plays in my knapsack: one written on a week's leave in India, and the other on a troopship between Bombay and Singapore.

I also returned to two other things I had left behind when leaving for India: a typewriter and a wife. The typewriter had come with her. Let me explain, before you jump to the conclusion that I married her for her Remington, that it was a totally unexpected wedding present—an old machine, remodeled, the only kind you could buy in wartime, and in her and my terms wildly expensive. The typewriter, which was still in use as late as 1958, was an act of faith, a practical expression of confidence, like the room I discovered set by for me in the place she had found for us to live when, this five years later, I got back from India. There are talents which not only survive but thrive on opposition and neglect. I have never had to ask myself whether mine would have been one of them.

But there must have been times during the next four long years—they seemed so much longer—when she asked herself whether her confidence had been misplaced. I know there must have been, not because she showed it, but because I asked myself the same question.

When I arrived home in June 1946, I had three months paid release leave ahead of me and we had a little place to live. We never discussed my getting a job. I dashed around seeing, or trying to see, the people I imagined must know who I was. I studied the market. I wrote articles and stories. I saw people who had been concerned with the Anglo-Palestinian play competition. One of them introduced me to an agent. She took me on. She didn't like either of the plays I'd brought back, but I was already at work on another.

Before the three months was quite up, my wife said she hoped I didn't mind but that it seemed she was slightly pregnant. There were only two answers to that. The first was that I didn't mind at all; the second was to present myself at a place called The London Appointments Board, which was a kind of labor exchange for people who had held emergency commissions.

Noting that I'd been an audit clerk, the lady said she had the perfect job for me, at six pounds a week, with the merchant bankers, Brown Shipley. I said merchant banking wasn't quite me because I really wanted to be a writer. She said that this seemed to indicate that I hadn't quite readjusted to civilian life and that she would recommend me to the accounts department of the headquarters of the R.A.F. Malcolm Club in Belgravia. I said Belgravia sounded quite nice, so that's where I went.

The joke about the R.A.F. Malcolm Club was that everyone who turned up there to help with the accounts had been offered Brown Shipley. Subsequently in my professional life, I was always meeting men who had been invited to join that estimable firm, but it is only about three years ago that I discovered who had done so. And then I wondered whether I had been wise to decline the opportunity. The ex-officer who did *not* decline was Lieutenant-Colonel Heath, known to us all as Ted. And we all know how well *that* boy has done for himself.

And come to think of it, if *Chambers Dictionary* is to be relied on, and there is really an opening here for someone at the organ or the piano, has your committee, I wonder, made the right appointment?

Have you ever looked back on your life and thought how logical its pattern is in retrospect, how no experience—however tiresome—is ever wasted? How even the discordant notes are rearranged eventually into a kind of harmony? I had never felt like an accountant, but had acquired some useful basic qualifications. I had wanted to be a poet—now knew I wasn't. But the young officer who had thought I was and had published me, one of the people I'd called on to no avail, and who was now a publisher, suddenly wanted me—not as a poet, but as a bookkeeper. He had remembered that I was at least qualified as that, rang me, and in a brace of shakes, had hired me.

I entered publishing. If keeping books was the only way I could earn a living, then at least here I was keeping the books of a firm whose business was central to my life. And I was, if you will allow me to say so, a very good bookkeeper. As the publishing firm grew, so did my status. From bookkeeper to accountant, from accountant to chief accountant, from chief accountant to finance manager, from finance manager to company secretary of first one, and then four associated publishing companies.

Mind you, my salary did not actually reflect this proliferation of dignities and responsibilities, and there was never at any stage more than one person in the accounts department. Me. This young officer who controlled the firms had delusions of grandeur, and towards the end his interests extended to fields far from literature. Or perhaps not so far—he owned a whiskey firm. But he was also a member of Parliament. I will not, perhaps need not, say for which party.

And there came a time—four years later, in 1950—when I felt, as an officer of these companies, that I had to stop thinking in the short term of my security, of my wife, my children, and my mortgage, and take a long hard look at the organization which employed me.

Having done so, I resigned. I gave the three months notice necessary under my contract of service. An attempt was now made to get rid of me at once, without notice or pay. I said I was willing to go, so long as a banker's order was made out to ensure my contracted salary. Result—some bluster from the officer's father, who was also an accountant. But I had not read the laws of contract for nothing. Final result: banker's order. Three months paid separation leave.

You may think I was unwise. My wife didn't think I was unwise. We celebrated by going to Paris for a week. We couldn't really afford it, but it seemed right. When I got back, I admit I wondered whether I hadn't been hasty. Events proved I had really only been just in time. Three years and seven company secretaries later, the firm went bankrupt and the young M.P. went to prison for seven years for forgery. He is many years dead, which is why I can speak about it. There was a great opportunity there—we had a good list and we were full of enthusiasm. Many of my colleagues who underwent that same traumatic experience have, I'm glad to say, prospered. For instance, the young man who handled the advertising is now the editorial director of the firm that publishes me.

But, even if you're not wondering why I threw over a job, you may be wondering what happened to that enthusiastic writer during the four years he spent in the thick of the commercial side of the literary world. The answer is that he had been writing plays, one after the other—thinking about them in spare moments, month after month, and then getting to the point of having to write them down, also in his spare moments. Writing them down, typing them out, sending them to his agent. Basking in her praise, sharing her hopes, setting out after office hours trembling with expectation to meet an interested producer in St. Martin's Lane, or travelling on a Saturday morning to meet the television drama pandits at Alexandra Palace. Or, once, rushing to the phone because his wife had run upstairs, also trembling, and whispered, "It's Margaret Rawlings."

Do I need to go on? Of course I don't. Perhaps you *all* know it. The terrible cumulative weight of sustained failure. The only thing that hadn't failed was my inner conviction. And now I had three paid months of holiday ahead.

One thing I had done, at last, before leaving the publishing house, was sit down, the previous autumn, and write a novel. My agent had begun offering this, and by the time I left the publishing firm it had already been rejected several times.

Now I sat down and tried my hand at something new. A ninety-minute radio play. It only took me three days. When my wife had read it she said, "That's the best thing you have ever done." She was right. Do you know why? Because it was written direct out of experience, and whatever voice I had, which was mine alone, at last came through. My agent was also enthusiastic. But the principal effect on me, of having written it, was to make me realize that the play was only a preliminary skirmish round a subject for a novel. I began the novel at once.

So let me take stock of the situation in this summer of 1950. I had a novel going the rounds, a radio play on its way to the B.B.C., and a new novel on the stocks, but no job in prospect. A job came more or less out of the blue. I won't bore you with the details, although I'll gladly answer questions about it later. In retrospect I see that it fitted into the logical pattern of my life.

In short, I was invited by the senior partner of a leading firm of authors' agents to go in and learn the business. What he offered me in fact was not just a job but prospects of partnership and eventual succession. I had never thought of being an agent—I'm not sure that anybody ever does—but looked at purely as a job, it attracted me because it would keep me in the world I knew I wished to live in—the world of books. Looked at as a prospect, it seemed formidable but challenging. I was thirty. My own writing had more or less failed. It would have been rather silly to turn the offer down. I joined the firm in October of 1950.

Ten years later, after a lot of heart searching, but with the greatest mutual goodwill, and I think mutual affection, this man and I ended what had indeed become a partnership—not because I was now making so much money from my own work that I couldn't spare the time to manage other people's—far,

far from that—but because, at the age of 40, I knew that the energy needed to go on doing two jobs was at last beginning to flag. A computer calculating the risks would have said, stay with the agency and let the writing gradually fade away.

I made the other decision. In severely practical terms it wasn't sensible, but writers are not awfully sensible people. Again, I must say, it was a decision I couldn't have made without support at home. Those ten years as an agent were the only ones we have spent bolstered by a sense of security. They also, by chance, coincided with the first years of being bolstered by the kind of successes that seem to wipe out the years of failure and near-despair, which nearly every writer knows all too well. Successes which I like to think come nevertheless to everyone who— as Mrs. Wallin so wisely advocated in her article in this autumn's review—*perseveres and refuses to be downhearted for long.*

I think it is true to say that every author remembers very clearly the moment when he receives proof at last that he has broken through that seemingly impenetrable barrier that separates or seems to separate the aspiring from the proven writer, the amateur from the professional. I certainly remember my own moment.

I was in the loo.

Now my wife is not in the habit of pushing letters under the door of the smallest room, and the appearance of a small white rectangle, coming apparently from nowhere, was a suitably mystical experience. She had made an exception because the envelope was from the B.B.C. She knew I had already talked to a producer about my radio play, and that I pretended to expect that nothing would come of it.

The letter was not from the producer, but from the contracts department. All I now had to do to prove I was a writer was sign on the dotted line. And jolly well get ninety guineas into the bargain. I stared at this letter and contract for some time.

After that the image fades. You could say that an amateur went into the closet and that a professional emerged. Although that of course would mean that the amateur, the aspiring young writer, by then a scarred veteran of thirty years, is still ensconced there. I have often wondered in fact whether the people who now live in that house have ever felt, in that closet, a curious emanation for which there is no accounting, a sense of delight so profound that it can only be called tranquillity, so that they find themselves spending longer there than is either seemly or necessary, simply to enjoy this rare, this elusive aroma of peace from another world.

And I think, in autobiographical terms, that is more or less the place to leave me. It is certainly how I should like you to think of your president—and of his wife—who understood the importance of that little white rectangle. But the story is true.

Before I close though, and answer what I hope will be a great number of questions, there is just one other autobiographical note.

If you know me at all, you will know me as a novelist, and you may be wondering what happened to the novel that was on offer before I wrote the radio play. The answer is *nothing*. It was declined by seventeen publishers. The seventeenth were Eyre and Spottiswoode, who rang my agent early in 1951 and said "Yes, we could publish this and not be ashamed, but we're not going to. We have an idea that it's not how the author will write in future, so we're sending it back and expressing interest in his future work."

Now—and this is the point—I hadn't *waited* to find out what seventeen publishers thought of it. I'd written the radio play, and got on with the next novel, an expansion of the play. My agent was therefore able to say to Eyre and Spottiswoode, "Would you like to see something of the novel he's writing now? I believe it's about halfway finished, and I know it's an expansion of the theme of a radio play that's just been accepted by the B.B.C."

Well, what could they say? They said yes, they would be willing to look at the unfinished novel. And the result was that I had the very odd experience of signing a contract for what ranks as my first novel before it was even finished, and with money coming to me not only on delivery but on signature. The motto of this story is, *keep going*. Even an unpublished author is in business. And he needs his stock in trade.

But what I am very aware of is how often in my life, unfailingly, there have been people who have made me feel that it would be worth my while to keep going. To persevere. Perhaps there are people here who have never had, and still have not got, people close to them who are willing to tell them that. And I know that that must be very hard.

Hard, particularly, though, because it emphasizes how completely alone every writer is, however much encouragement he gets. At the moment of writing he *is* alone. No one can really help him at that moment. It has to come from inside. In that regard, everyone in this room faces the same problem. But the existence of circles such as this does help every one of us to face up to it, and so I feel not only honored by your committee's invitation—which having formally accepted I now publicly thank them for—but I also feel encouraged myself, as a writer, to be here, with the opportunity to talk about the things that matter to all of us.

Notes for Talk and Reading at Stamford Grammar School

◆

[*At the request of Mrs. Avery-Scott's nephew Hugh Allen, a teacher at the Stamford Grammar School in Lincolnshire, Scott agreed to speak to the students there on March 18, 1975, about the writing of fiction. The notes he made for that talk, except for comments in his letters, comprise his only public statements about* The Raj Quartet *after he finished the last volume of that tetralogy. First Scott gives some general comments about fiction, then he briefly looks at the entire Quartet and speaks about its point of view and overall organization. While these are only notes, they are illuminating and suggestive about* The Quartet.]

General points: My idea of *what a novel is*:

From Bergonzi: It is a *book*: "A small hard rectangular object, whose pages are bound along one edge into fixed covers and numbered consecutively."

From W. Allen: "An extended metaphor of its author's view of life."

On Writing and the Novel

Myself: A series of *images*, conveyed from me to you, in such a manner that my view of life is also conveyed—BUT ONLY TO ONE PERSON AT A TIME: THE READER (consenting adults). *IT IS THAT READER I'M WRITING TO.*

The small hard rectangular object is the prison in which the novelist works—the poet need not, and the dramatist doesn't.

Importance to us of the book (writer-to-reader).

Audio-visual-tactile-cultural—as danger to critical response (Leavis on criticism: "This is so, isn't it? Yes, but . . .").

Beginning a novel (two ways):

Image floating into mind.
Having an idea of writing a book on a particular subject. Won't begin until the images start coming.

Quote Fowles on *French Lieutenant's Woman.*

Mention Conrad: Lord Jim. Podmore Williams. The Jeddah incident. Seeing Williams in Singapore. Sixteen years later writes Lord Jim.
The Raj Quartet: Going to India in 1964. No idea why, except to recharge batteries.
1919: Amritsar. Miss Sherwood.
1942: Quit India riots (imprisonment of Indian leaders, Gandhi, etc.).
1964: Seeing the anglicized Indian and the Australian girl.
May 1964: Girl suddenly becomes Daphne Manners and the man Hari Kumar. Time August 8, 1942. Like Miss Sherwood, she has been attacked. Hari arrested.
Even so, the novel can't begin until I see this imaged out.

The question of who is telling the story:

A variable stumbling block. *Only important to the writer so that he can convince himself of his narrative.*

212

NOTES FOR TALK AND READING

Third person: omniscience unless written from point of view of only one person.

Second person: "You did this. You thought that." *Terribly awkward.*

First person: Popular with authors but limiting. Anyway the "I" has to be a character too.

Raj Device:

Use of The Writer—sometimes called The Stranger or The Traveler (according to circumstances). Rare appearances, but allows for the flexibility needed in this four-volume history of an age and a period.
Interviews, letters, extracts from works or accounts written or tape-recorded by the characters (who have been approached for information) plus the writer's own *reconstructions.*
The writer, not precisely me, so that I manage to achieve *detachment* as well as involvement.

Read first paragraph of *Jewel in the Crown:* Throwing the image at the reader. But already you can see that another character, Miss Crane, has been created and given some significance. (Historically, she is closer to Miss Sherwood than even Daphne is—a missionary.)

Check through part headings of *Jewel:* Miss Crane/The MacGregor House (read first paragraph) Sister Ludmila (mixture of history and interview). An Evening at the Club (writer recording his evening there in 1964, with survivors of 1942)./ Young Kumar (straightforward reconstruction)./ Civil and Military—exchanges with a civil servant, plus Military Reminiscence, which set *the writer off on the trail.*/ The Bibighar Gardens —Daphne Manners's written confession.

Read end, which shows stranger already aware that there is *more to tell* (from page 448: "Imagine then a flat landscape . . ." and page 450: "a girl admirably suited to her surroundings where there is always the promise of a story continuing instead of finishing."

No idea that there would be *four novels.*

Problems of keeping each self-contained but related to the whole.
Invention of new characters in each to carry the weight of the book—seeing the central situation from different angles. But still using the writer or stranger or traveler as the hidden narrative device.

Read opening paragraphs of *The Day of the Scorpion.* But virtually the whole of this book is a reconstruction—ordinary narrative. It has been established, at least in the author's mind, that a man has been traveling round India and England collecting information from people.

Politically, the Quartet now opens out congress muslim, military family, princely India. Hill Station.

When it comes to the *Towers of Silence,* the Quartet narrows down again to a woman similar to Miss Crane, an old missionary, Barbie Batchelor, retired to a hill station.

One can write, and believe it thus:
"In September 1939—" etc. (Read first paragraph of *Towers of Silence.*)
The Quartet has, step by step, narrowed itself down to the viewpoint of a single character.
She certainly brings the whole thing to a close because she is out of the running by 1944.

Problems of the last novel in the sequence:

A breath of fresh air: Perron (also modernity),
Purvis (political thing).

Slightly cynical tone needed—also dramatized illustration of English ignorance of India.

Plus the need to convey the political historical movement without appearing to be writing just history.

Cynical tone: First paragraph (also establishes historical context).

Ignorance: pages 8–9.

NOTES FOR TALK AND READING

Introducing the "breath of fresh air"—Perron
(page 11: "In the first six months . . .")

Read Purvis and Perron: page 31 on.

Note the reversal at the end of the chapter—the slight change of tone from comedy to tragicomedy.
>   Evening at the Maharanee's—straight narrative.
>   Journeys into Uneasy Distances:
>>   Again the stranger enters as (passenger).
>   Read first paragraph.
>>   Note flexibility of this method—the transition from end of paragraph on page 113 to the new section leading us back to the historical moment of Sarah and her father returning to Ranpur and Pankot.

The Moghul room:	First-person narration by Guy Perron *re* his stay in Pankot in 1945.
The Dak bungalow:	First-person narration by Sarah Layton.
The Circuit House:	Reconstruction of M. A. Kasim's meeting with his son.
Pandora's box:	Reconstruction of Perron's visit to India just before partition and independence.

Again, how do you convey the history: cartoonist device: an unexpected development of the casual use of a cartoonist on the first three pages of the book.

Rounding the imagery of the book off: equally unexpected but fortunate use of an earlier bit of casual imagery—Gaffur the Poet. Read final poem. (All the last lines refer to other imagery.)

Graces bestowed: Meaning of name Daphne. Recollection of Philoctetes the Great Archer (Hari).

Why do I write about *India?* (Walter Allen's metaphor)

>   Read from: *Essays by Divers Hands*
>>   *The Raj*
>>   and *Division*—The bones of the face, page 103

>   Final reading from *The Corrida at San Feliu*—re the duende.

INDEX

◆

INDEX